Iraqi
Cookbook
Authentic Recipes

UNCOVER THE RICH AND DIVERSE FLAVORS OF IRAQ

ZAHRA H. FARHAN

IRAQI COOKBOOK
Uncover the Rich and Diverse Flavors of Iraq.

© Zahra H. Farhan
© E.G.P. Editorial
   ISBN-13: 9798879960105

FLAVOURS THAT
CROSS BORDERS

From my earliest memories, the tales and songs of Iraq were a constant backdrop, cultivating a profound bond with my ancestral land despite being far from where my grandparents were born. My grandparents, embodiments of relentless ambition and boundless hope, chose during the 1950s to migrate to London, driven by the desire for a better future for their descendants. They became an integral part of London's vibrant Iraqi community, enriching it with their culture and dreams.

The journey to establish themselves in a new country was daunting, but my grandparents' unwavering courage and optimism never faltered. Their stories emphasized the significance of maintaining our cultural heritage, especially through the tradition of cooking. My grandmother's kitchen was a sanctuary filled with the aromas and tastes of dishes like masgouf, dolma, and kubba, which served not only as nourishment for our bodies but also as a link to our Iraqi heritage.

My grandmother believed that cooking was more than just preparing meals; it was an act of love, a way to preserve our history, and a means to share our narrative with future generations. Every recipe she passed down was laced with anecdotes, insights, and memories of Iraq, making each dish a celebration of our identity.

The role of Iraqi cuisine in my life was not only shaped by my grandmother's teachings but also by cookbooks from Egypt that highlighted the richness and diversity of Middle Eastern culinary traditions. These books helped my grandmother to perfect her recipes, which became the highlights of our family gatherings in London.

Now, as an author, I am driven to keep my grandmother's culinary legacy alive. Though she is no longer with us, her spirit and teachings continue to inspire me every time I recreate one of her signature dishes. This book is a tribute to her, a testament to her life's resilience, love, and passion for cooking, aiming to inspire others to discover the joy and unity found in the culinary arts.

With this book, my goal is for readers to not only learn how to prepare authentic Iraqi dishes but also to feel the affection and dedication my grandmother put into every recipe. This work seeks to bridge generations and cultures, illustrating that cooking can be a haven for the heart and soul, regardless of where we find ourselves.

TABLE OF CONTENTS

APPETIZIERS

Appetizers in Iraqi cuisine are not merely introductory dishes; they are a vibrant showcase of the country's rich culinary heritage, setting the stage for the meal to come. These starter dishes are renowned for their diverse flavors and textures, offering a glimpse into the depth of Iraqi culinary traditions. With ingredients that range from vegetables and legumes to meats and spices, Iraqi appetizers are a testament to the cuisine's versatility and its ability to cater to a wide array of palates.

Nutritionally, Iraqi starters are designed to be both enticing and health-conscious, incorporating an abundance of fresh produce, whole grains, and lean proteins. This thoughtful composition ensures that each appetizer not only tantalizes the taste buds but also contributes to a balanced diet. The careful balance of spices and herbs used in these dishes not only enhances flavor but also offers various health benefits, supporting overall well-being.

The role of appetizers in Iraqi cuisine extends beyond merely whetting the appetite; they are an integral part of the dining experience, encouraging communal dining and conversation. Their versatility allows them to be enjoyed in various settings, making them perfect for both everyday meals and special occasions.

TABBOULEH

Ingredients

- Bulgur - 1/2 cup.
- Fresh parsley, finely chopped - 2 cups.
- Mint leaves, finely chopped - 1/4 cup.
- Tomatoes, finely diced - 3 medium.

- Cucumber, finely diced - 1 medium.
- Green onions, finely sliced - 3.
- Lemon juice - 1/4 cup.
- Extra virgin olive oil - 1/3 cup.
- Salt - to taste.
- Black pepper - to taste.

Instructions

1. Soak the bulgur in cold water for about 30 minutes until softened. Drain and squeeze out excess water.

2. In a large mixing bowl, combine the softened bulgur, parsley, mint, tomatoes, cucumber, and green onions.

3. In a small bowl, whisk together the lemon juice, olive oil, salt, and pepper. Pour over the salad and mix well.

4. Refrigerate for at least one hour to allow flavors to meld. Serve chilled.

HUMMUS

Ingredients

- Chickpeas, cooked and drained - 2 cups.
- Tahini - 1/2 cup.
- Lemon juice - 1/4 cup.
- Garlic, minced - 2 cloves.
- Extra virgin olive oil - 1/4 cup.
- Salt - to taste.
- Ground cumin - 1 tsp.
- Paprika - for garnish.

Instructions

1. In a food processor, blend the chickpeas, tahini, lemon

juice, garlic, olive oil, salt, and cumin until smooth.

2. If the mixture is too thick, add a little water or more olive oil to reach desired consistency.

3. Taste and adjust seasoning if necessary.

4. Transfer to a serving dish, drizzle with olive oil, and sprinkle with paprika. Serve with pita bread or fresh vegetables.

BABA GHANOUSH

Ingredients

- Eggplants - 2 large.
- Tahini - 1/4 cup.
- Lemon juice - 3 tbsp.
- Garlic, minced - 2 cloves.
- Extra virgin olive oil - 2 tbsp.
- Salt - to taste.
- Ground cumin - 1/2 tsp.
- Parsley, chopped - for garnish.

Instructions

1. Preheat the oven to 400°F (200°C). Pierce the eggplants with a fork and place on a baking sheet. Roast until tender, about 40 minutes.

2. Once cool, peel the skin off the eggplants and place the flesh in a colander to drain excess water.

3. In a food processor, combine the eggplant flesh, tahini, lemon juice, garlic, olive oil, salt, and cumin. Blend until smooth.

4. Taste and adjust seasoning if necessary.

5. Transfer to a serving dish, drizzle with olive oil, and garnish with parsley. Serve with pita bread or fresh vegetables.

FALAFEL

Ingredients

- Chickpeas, dried - 1 cup.
- Onion, chopped - 1 medium.
- Parsley, chopped - 1/4 cup.
- Garlic, minced - 3 cloves.
- Cumin - 1 tsp.
- Coriander - 1 tsp.
- Salt - 1 tsp.
- Baking powder - 1/2 tsp.
- Flour - 2 tbsp.
- Oil - for frying.

Instructions

1. Soak the chickpeas overnight in water. Drain and rinse.

2. In a food processor, combine the chickpeas, onion, parsley, garlic, cumin, coriander, and salt. Process until blended but not pureed.

3. Stir in the baking powder and flour until the mixture can be shaped into balls. If it's too wet, add a little more flour.

4. Form the mixture into small balls and flatten slightly.

5. Heat oil in a deep fryer or large pan to 375°F (190°C). Fry the falafel in batches until golden brown, about 5 minutes.

6. Drain on paper towels. Serve hot with tahini sauce or wrapped in pita bread with vegetables.

KIBBEH

Ingredients

- Bulgur - 1 cup.
- Ground lamb - 1 lb.
- Onion, finely chopped - 1 large.
- Pine nuts - 1/4 cup.
- Allspice - 1 tsp.
- Salt - to taste.
- Pepper - to taste.
- Cinnamon - 1/2 tsp.
- Cayenne pepper - a pinch.
- Oil - for frying.

Instructions

1. Soak the bulgur in cold water for 30 minutes. Drain thoroughly.

2. In a large bowl, mix the bulgur, half of the ground lamb, onion, and seasonings. Process in batches in a food processor until well blended.

3. Cook the remaining ground lamb in a skillet with a little oil, add pine nuts, allspice, salt, and pepper. Cook until the lamb is browned.

4. Take a small amount of the bulgur mixture, flatten it in your hand, place a spoonful of the cooked lamb mixture in the center, and shape into balls or ovals.

5. Heat oil in a deep fryer or large pan to 375°F (190°C). Fry the kibbeh in batches until golden brown, about 5 minutes.

6. Drain on paper towels. Serve hot with yogurt or tahini sauce.

DOLMA (STUFFED GRAPE LEAVES)

Ingredients

- Grape leaves - 30 leaves.
- Rice, short-grain - 1 cup.
- Ground lamb - 1/2 pound.
- Onion, finely chopped - 1 medium.
- Parsley, chopped - 1/4 cup.
- Mint, dried - 1 tbsp.
- Tomato paste - 2 tbsp.
- Lemon juice - 1/4 cup.
- Extra virgin olive oil - 2 tbsp.
- Salt - to taste.
- Black pepper - to taste.

Instructions

1. Blanch the grape leaves in boiling water for 2-3 minutes, then rinse under cold water and drain.

2. Mix the rice, ground lamb, onion, parsley, mint, tomato paste, lemon juice, olive oil, salt, and pepper in a bowl.

3. Place a grape leaf on a flat surface, vein side up, and put about a tablespoon of the filling near the stem end.

4. Fold in the sides of the leaf over the filling, then roll tightly towards the top.

5. Arrange the stuffed leaves in a pot, seam-side down, in layers. Pour over enough water to cover, add a little more lemon juice and olive oil.

6. Place a plate on top to keep them submerged, then bring to a boil, reduce the heat, and simmer for about 45 minutes.

7. Serve warm or at room temperature.

FATTOUSH

Ingredients

- Romaine lettuce - 1 head, chopped.
- Cucumbers - 2, diced.
- Tomatoes - 3, diced.
- Radishes - 5, sliced.
- Green onions - 3, chopped.
- Pita bread - 2, toasted and broken into pieces.
- Mint leaves - 1/4 cup, chopped.
- Sumac - 2 tsp.
- Lemon juice - 1/4 cup.
- Extra virgin olive oil - 1/3 cup.
- Salt - to taste.
- Pepper - to taste.

Instructions

1. In a large salad bowl, combine the lettuce, cucumbers, tomatoes, radishes, green onions, pita pieces, and mint.

2. In a small bowl, whisk together the sumac, lemon juice, olive oil, salt, and pepper to make the dressing.

3. Pour the dressing over the salad and toss well to coat.

4. Serve immediately to keep the pita pieces crisp.

MUHAMMARA

Ingredients

- Roasted red peppers - 1 cup.
- Walnuts - 1/2 cup, toasted.
- Breadcrumbs - 1/4 cup.
- Garlic - 2 cloves, minced.
- Pomegranate molasses - 2 tbsp.
- Extra virgin olive oil - 1/4 cup.
- Lemon juice - 1 tbsp.
- Ground cumin - 1 tsp.
- Salt - to taste.
- Chili flakes - 1/2 tsp (optional).

Instructions

1. In a food processor, combine the roasted red peppers, walnuts, breadcrumbs, garlic, pomegranate molasses, olive oil, lemon juice, cumin, salt, and chili flakes.

2. Blend until smooth, scraping down the sides as necessary.

3. Adjust seasoning to taste, adding more salt or lemon juice if needed.

4. Transfer to a serving bowl and refrigerate for at least an hour before serving to allow flavors to meld.

5. Serve with pita bread or as a dip for vegetables.

SAMOON (IRAQI BREAD) WITH CHEESE

Ingredients

- Samoon bread - 4 pieces.
- Feta cheese - 1 cup, crumbled.
- Mozzarella cheese - 1 cup, shredded.
- Olive oil - 2 tbsp.
- Za'atar - 2 tsp.
- Fresh thyme leaves - 1 tbsp.

Instructions

1. Preheat the oven to 350°F (175°C).

2. Cut the samoon bread horizontally without going all the way through, creating a pocket.

3. Mix the feta and mozzarella cheeses in a bowl.

4. Stuff the cheese mixture into the bread pockets, drizzle with olive oil, and sprinkle with za'atar and thyme.

5. Place the stuffed bread on a baking sheet and bake for 10-12 minutes until the cheese is melted and the bread is crispy.

6. Serve warm.

BALANGOOSH

Ingredients

- Eggplants - 2 large, peeled and diced.
- Tomatoes - 2 large, diced.
- Onion - 1 large, chopped.
- Garlic - 3 cloves, minced.

- Green bell pepper - 1, diced.
- Tomato paste - 2 tbsp.
- Vegetable oil - 1/4 cup.
- Salt - to taste.
- Black pepper - to taste.
- Cumin - 1 tsp.
- Water - 1/2 cup.

Instructions

1. Heat the oil in a large skillet over medium heat. Add the onion and garlic, and sauté until soft.

2. Add the eggplants, tomatoes, green bell pepper, tomato paste, salt, pepper, cumin, and water.

3. Cover and simmer over low heat for 20-25 minutes, stirring occasionally, until the vegetables are tender.

4. Adjust the seasoning as needed and serve warm as a side dish or appetizer.

SAMBUSAK

Ingredients

- All-purpose flour - 2 cups.
- Yeast - 1 tsp.
- Warm water - 3/4 cup.
- Salt - 1/2 tsp.
- Sugar - 1 tsp.
- Ground lamb or beef - 1 lb.
- Onion, finely chopped - 1.
- Pine nuts - 1/4 cup.
- Allspice - 1 tsp.
- Cinnamon - 1/4 tsp.
- Salt - to taste.

- Vegetable oil - for frying.

Instructions

1. Dissolve yeast and sugar in warm water, let it sit for 10 minutes until frothy.

2. In a large bowl, mix flour and salt. Add the yeast mixture and knead to form a smooth dough. Cover and let it rise for 1 hour.

3. For the filling, sauté onion and pine nuts in a bit of oil until onions are soft. Add the meat, allspice, cinnamon, and salt. Cook until browned.

4. Roll out the dough and cut into circles. Place a spoonful of filling on each circle, fold over, and seal the edges.

5. Heat oil in a deep fryer or pan and fry the sambusak until golden brown on both sides.

6. Drain on paper towels and serve hot.

IRAQI PICKLES

Ingredients

- Cucumbers - 1 kg.
- Carrots - 2, sliced.
- Green chilies - 5.
- Garlic cloves - 10.
- Water - 4 cups.
- Vinegar - 1 cup.
- Salt - 3 tbsp.
- Sugar - 1 tsp.

Instructions

1. Sterilize jars and lids by boiling them in water for 10 minutes.

2. In a large pot, bring water, vinegar, salt, and sugar to a boil.

3. Pack cucumbers, carrots, chilies, and garlic into the jars.

4. Pour the boiling vinegar mixture over the vegetables, leaving a 1/2 inch of headspace.

5. Seal the jars and process them in a boiling water bath for 10 minutes.

6. Let the pickles sit for at least two weeks before consuming for best flavor.

MASGOUF TARTARE

Ingredients

- Fresh carp fillet, minced - 1 lb.
- Tomatoes, finely chopped - 2.
- Onion, finely minced - 1.
- Cilantro, chopped - 1/4 cup.
- Lemon juice - 3 tbsp.
- Olive oil - 2 tbsp.
- Salt - to taste.
- Black pepper - to taste.

Instructions

1. In a mixing bowl, combine the minced carp, tomatoes, onion, and cilantro.

2. Add lemon juice, olive oil, salt, and pepper. Mix well.

3. Taste and adjust seasoning if necessary.

4. Refrigerate for at least 1 hour to allow flavors to meld.

5. Serve chilled, garnished with extra cilantro or lemon slices.

EGGPLANT MAKDOUS

Ingredients

- Small eggplants - 10.
- Walnuts, chopped - 1 cup.
- Garlic cloves, minced - 10.
- Red chili powder - 1 tsp.
- Olive oil - as needed.
- Salt - to taste.

Instructions

1. Cut a slit in each eggplant and soak them in salted water for 12 hours to remove bitterness.

2. Drain and squeeze out excess water from the eggplants.

3. Mix walnuts, garlic, chili powder, and salt for the filling.

4. Stuff the eggplants with the walnut mixture.

5. Place the stuffed eggplants in a jar and cover with olive oil.

6. Seal the jar and let it sit for at least one week before consuming.

LABNEH WITH IRAQI SPICES

Ingredients

- Labneh - 2 cups.
- Za'atar - 2 tbsp.
- Sumac - 1 tsp.
- Olive oil - 1/4 cup.
- Mint, dried - 1 tsp.
- Salt - to taste.
- Garlic, minced - 1 clove.

Instructions

1. In a bowl, mix labneh with za'atar, sumac, mint, salt, and garlic.

2. Drizzle olive oil over the mixture and mix well.

3. Refrigerate for 1 hour before serving to allow flavors to develop.

4. Serve with pita bread or as a dip for vegetables.

SOUPS

Soups within Iraqi cuisine occupy a special place, acting as a warm invitation to the rich tapestry of flavors and traditions that define this culinary culture. Each soup recipe tells a story of heritage and home, blending spices, grains, and meats in a way that nourishes the soul as much as the body. This variety showcases the adaptability of Iraqi cooking, offering something for every taste preference, from the hearty richness of meat-based broths to the light and refreshing zest of vegetable purees.

Nutrition plays a pivotal role in the composition of Iraqi soups, with a focus on ingredients that offer a symphony of benefits to one's health. Legumes, vegetables, and lean meats form the cornerstone of these dishes, providing essential nutrients in a digestible and soothing form. The inclusion of spices not only enriches the flavor profile but also introduces antioxidants and anti-inflammatory properties, supporting a diet that promotes wellness.

The essence of soups in Iraqi cuisine lies in their ability to bring people together, serving as a comforting starter that opens both appetite and conversation. Their versatility makes them a staple for both everyday dining and celebratory feasts, underscoring their integral role in a nutritious and culturally rich diet.

SHORBAT ADAS (LENTIL SOUP)

Ingredients

- Red lentils - 1 cup.
- Water - 4 cups.
- Carrot, diced - 1.
- Onion, chopped - 1.

- Garlic cloves, minced - 2.
- Cumin - 1 tsp.
- Turmeric - 1/2 tsp.
- Salt - to taste.
- Lemon juice - 2 tbsp.
- Olive oil - 2 tbsp.

Instructions

1. Rinse the lentils in cold water until the water runs clear.

2. In a large pot, heat the olive oil over medium heat. Add the onions and garlic, sautéing until soft.

3. Add the carrots, lentils, cumin, turmeric, and salt to the pot. Stir to combine.

4. Add the water and bring to a boil. Reduce heat to low, cover, and simmer for about 20-25 minutes, until the lentils are soft.

5. Use an immersion blender to puree the soup to your desired consistency. Stir in the lemon juice.

6. Serve hot, garnished with a drizzle of olive oil or fresh parsley if desired.

BAMYIA (OKRA SOUP)

Ingredients

- Okra, fresh or frozen - 2 cups.
- Lamb or beef, cubed - 1 lb.
- Tomato paste - 2 tbsp.
- Garlic cloves, minced - 3.
- Onion, chopped - 1.

- Coriander powder - 1 tsp.
- Lemon juice - 2 tbsp.
- Salt - to taste.
- Black pepper - to taste.
- Water - 6 cups.
- Olive oil - 2 tbsp.

Instructions

1. In a large pot, heat the olive oil over medium heat. Add the onions and garlic, sautéing until they turn translucent.

2. Add the meat and brown on all sides.

3. Stir in the tomato paste, coriander, salt, and pepper. Cook for 2 minutes.

4. Add the water and bring to a boil. Reduce the heat to low, cover, and simmer until the meat is tender, about 1 hour.

5. Add the okra and lemon juice to the pot. Simmer for an additional 20 minutes or until the okra is tender.

6. Adjust the seasoning and serve hot with rice or bread.

SHORBAT BAZELLA (PEA SOUP)

Ingredients

- Green peas, fresh or frozen - 2 cups.
- Carrot, diced - 1.
- Potato, diced - 1.
- Onion, chopped - 1.
- Garlic cloves, minced - 2.
- Vegetable broth - 4 cups.

- Cumin - 1 tsp.
- Salt - to taste.
- Black pepper - to taste.
- Olive oil - 1 tbsp.

Instructions

1. In a large pot, heat the olive oil over medium heat. Add the onions and garlic, sautéing until soft.

2. Add the carrots, potatoes, peas, cumin, salt, and pepper. Stir to combine.

3. Pour in the vegetable broth and bring to a boil. Reduce heat to low, cover, and simmer for 20-25 minutes, until vegetables are tender.

4. Use an immersion blender to puree the soup to your desired consistency.

5. Adjust the seasoning and serve hot, garnished with a drizzle of olive oil or fresh herbs if desired.

SHORBAT FASOULIA (BEAN SOUP)

Ingredients

- White beans, soaked overnight - 1 cup.
- Tomato, chopped - 1.
- Onion, chopped - 1.
- Garlic cloves, minced - 2.
- Carrot, diced - 1.
- Cumin - 1 tsp.
- Coriander - 1 tsp.
- Salt - to taste.
- Black pepper - to taste.
- Water - 6 cups.

- Olive oil - 2 tbsp.

Instructions

1. Rinse the soaked beans and drain.

2. In a large pot, heat the olive oil over medium heat. Add the onions, garlic, and carrots, sautéing until soft.

3. Add the beans, tomatoes, cumin, coriander, salt, pepper, and water to the pot.

4. Bring to a boil, then reduce heat to low, cover, and simmer for about 1.5 to 2 hours, or until the beans are tender.

5. Adjust the seasoning and serve hot, garnished with fresh parsley or coriander if desired.

SHORBAT CHARD (SWISS CHARD SOUP)

Ingredients

- Swiss chard, chopped - 2 cups.
- Onion, chopped - 1.
- Garlic cloves, minced - 2.
- Potato, diced - 1.
- Chicken or vegetable broth - 4 cups.
- Lemon juice - 2 tbsp.
- Salt - to taste.
- Black pepper - to taste.
- Olive oil - 1 tbsp.

Instructions

1. In a large pot, heat the olive oil over medium heat. Add the onions and garlic, sautéing until soft.

2. Add the potatoes and broth. Bring to a boil, then reduce heat to low and simmer until the potatoes are nearly tender, about 10 minutes.

3. Add the Swiss chard, salt, and pepper. Continue to simmer until the chard is wilted and the potatoes are fully tender, about 5 minutes more.

4. Stir in the lemon juice.

5. Adjust the seasoning and serve hot, garnished with a drizzle of olive oil if desired.

MARQAT FASOLIA (WHITE BEAN STEW)

Ingredients

- White beans - 2 cups.
- Lamb or beef, cubed - 1 lb.
- Onion, finely chopped - 1.
- Garlic cloves, minced - 2.
- Tomato paste - 2 tbsp.
- Tomatoes, diced - 2.
- Carrots, diced - 2.
- Potatoes, cubed - 2.
- Cumin - 1 tsp.
- Salt - to taste.
- Black pepper - to taste.
- Water - 6 cups.
- Olive oil - 2 tbsp.

Instructions

1. Soak the white beans overnight in water, then drain.

2. In a large pot, heat olive oil over medium heat. Add the onion and garlic, cooking until soft.

3. Add the meat and brown on all sides.

4. Stir in the tomato paste, diced tomatoes, cumin, salt, and pepper, cooking for a few minutes.

5. Add the soaked beans, carrots, potatoes, and water. Bring to a boil, then reduce heat, cover, and simmer until the beans and meat are tender, about 1.5 hours.

6. Adjust the seasoning as needed and serve hot.

SHORBAT KIFTA (MEATBALL SOUP)

Ingredients

- Ground lamb or beef - 1 lb.
- Rice, uncooked - 1/4 cup.
- Onion, grated - 1.
- Parsley, finely chopped - 1/4 cup.
- Salt - 1 tsp.
- Black pepper - 1/2 tsp.
- Chicken or beef broth - 6 cups.
- Tomato paste - 2 tbsp.
- Potatoes, cubed - 2.
- Carrots, sliced - 2.

Instructions

1. In a bowl, mix together the ground meat, rice, onion, parsley, salt, and pepper. Form into small meatballs.

2. In a large pot, bring the broth to a boil. Add the tomato paste, potatoes, and carrots. Simmer for 10 minutes.

3. Gently add the meatballs to the soup, one at a time. Reduce heat and simmer until the meatballs are cooked through and the vegetables are tender, about 25 minutes.

4. Adjust the seasoning to taste and serve hot.

SHORBAT RUMMAN (POMEGRANATE SOUP)

Ingredients

- Pomegranate juice - 4 cups.
- Yellow split peas - 1 cup.
- Onion, finely chopped - 1.
- Ground lamb or beef - 1/2 lb.
- Mint leaves, dried - 1 tbsp.
- Sugar - 2 tbsp.
- Salt - to taste.
- Black pepper - to taste.
- Water - 2 cups.

Instructions

1. Rinse the yellow split peas and soak in water for 30 minutes, then drain.

2. In a large pot, combine the pomegranate juice, water, and soaked split peas. Bring to a boil, then reduce heat and simmer until the peas are tender, about 1 hour.

3. In a skillet, cook the onion until soft. Add the ground meat, cooking until browned. Season with salt and pepper.

4. Add the meat mixture to the soup along with dried mint and sugar. Simmer for another 30 minutes.

5. Adjust the seasoning and serve hot, garnished with fresh mint if available.

SHORBA T'AMEYA (TOMATO SOUP)

Ingredients

- Tomatoes, pureed - 4 cups.
- Garlic cloves, minced - 2.
- Onion, finely chopped - 1.
- Vegetable broth - 4 cups.
- Cumin - 1 tsp.
- Coriander - 1 tsp.
- Salt - to taste.
- Black pepper - to taste.
- Olive oil - 2 tbsp.
- Fresh cilantro, chopped - for garnish.

Instructions

1. In a large pot, heat the olive oil over medium heat. Add the onion and garlic, cooking until the onion is soft.

2. Add the pureed tomatoes, cumin, coriander, salt, and pepper. Cook for a few minutes until the tomatoes are heated through.

3. Add the vegetable broth and bring to a boil. Reduce heat and simmer for 20-30 minutes.

4. Adjust the seasoning as needed. Serve hot, garnished with fresh cilantro.

KUBBEH HAMOUTH (SOUR KUBBEH SOUP)

Ingredients

- For the kubbeh:
- Bulgur wheat - 1 cup.
- Ground beef or lamb - 1/2 lb.

- Onion, minced - 1.
- Salt - 1/2 tsp.
- Black pepper - 1/4 tsp.
- For the soup:
- Chicken or beef broth - 6 cups.
- Lemon juice - 1/4 cup.
- Swiss chard, chopped - 2 cups.
- Beet greens, chopped - 1 cup (optional).
- Onion, chopped - 1.
- Garlic cloves, minced - 3.
- Salt - to taste.
- Black pepper - to taste.

Instructions

1. Prepare the kubbeh by mixing bulgur wheat, ground meat, onion, salt, and pepper. Form into small balls or ovals.

2. In a large pot, bring the broth to a boil. Add the kubbeh, onion, garlic, salt, and pepper. Reduce heat and simmer for 30 minutes.

3. Add the lemon juice, Swiss chard, and beet greens (if using). Cook until the greens are tender, about 10 minutes.

4. Adjust the seasoning and serve hot, offering a tangy and comforting soup.

CHICKEN AND VEGETABLE SOUP

Ingredients

- Chicken breast, cubed - 1 lb.
- Carrots, diced - 2.
- Potatoes, cubed - 2.

- Zucchini, sliced - 1.
- Onion, chopped - 1.
- Garlic cloves, minced - 2.
- Chicken broth - 6 cups.
- Olive oil - 2 tbsp.
- Salt - to taste.
- Black pepper - to taste.
- Cumin - 1 tsp.

Instructions

1. In a large pot, heat the olive oil over medium heat. Add the onion and garlic, sautéing until translucent.

2. Add the chicken and cook until it's no longer pink.

3. Add the carrots, potatoes, zucchini, chicken broth, salt, pepper, and cumin to the pot.

4. Bring to a boil, then reduce heat to low and simmer until vegetables are tender, about 20-25 minutes.

5. Adjust the seasoning to taste and serve hot.

SHORBAT ZUCCHINI

Ingredients

- Zucchini, chopped - 4 cups.
- Onion, chopped - 1.
- Garlic cloves, minced - 2.
- Vegetable broth - 4 cups.
- Heavy cream - 1/2 cup (optional).
- Olive oil - 2 tbsp.
- Salt - to taste.
- Black pepper - to taste.
- Nutmeg - a pinch.

Instructions

1. In a large pot, heat the olive oil over medium heat. Add the onion and garlic, sautéing until soft.

2. Add the zucchini and cook for about 5 minutes, stirring occasionally.

3. Pour in the vegetable broth, bring to a boil, then reduce heat and simmer until the zucchini is very tender, about 15 minutes.

4. Use an immersion blender to puree the soup until smooth.

5. Stir in the heavy cream (if using), season with salt, pepper, and a pinch of nutmeg.

6. Serve hot, garnished with fresh herbs or a drizzle of olive oil.

IRAQI FISH SOUP

Ingredients

- Fish fillets, cubed - 1 lb.
- Tomato, chopped - 1.
- Onion, chopped - 1.
- Garlic cloves, minced - 2.
- Potatoes, cubed - 2.
- Carrots, sliced - 2.
- Fish broth - 6 cups.
- Cumin - 1 tsp.
- Coriander - 1 tsp.
- Salt - to taste.
- Black pepper - to taste.
- Lemon juice - 2 tbsp.

Instructions

1. In a large pot, bring the fish broth to a boil. Add the onion, garlic, potatoes, and carrots. Cook until the vegetables are halfway done.

2. Add the fish, tomato, cumin, coriander, salt, and pepper to the pot. Reduce heat to low and simmer until the fish is cooked through, about 10-15 minutes.

3. Stir in the lemon juice just before serving.

4. Adjust the seasoning to taste and serve hot, garnished with fresh cilantro or parsley if desired.

MUSHROOM AND BARLEY SOUP

Ingredients

- Mushrooms, sliced - 2 cups.
- Barley - 1/2 cup.
- Carrot, diced - 1.
- Onion, chopped - 1.
- Garlic cloves, minced - 2.
- Vegetable broth - 6 cups.
- Thyme - 1 tsp.
- Salt - to taste.
- Black pepper - to taste.
- Olive oil - 2 tbsp.

Instructions

1. In a large pot, heat the olive oil over medium heat. Add the onion, garlic, and carrot, sautéing until the onion is translucent.

2. Add the mushrooms and cook until they start to release their juices.

3. Stir in the barley, thyme, salt, pepper, and vegetable broth.

4. Bring to a boil, then reduce heat to low, cover, and simmer until the barley is tender, about 45 minutes to 1 hour.

5. Adjust the seasoning to taste and serve hot.

LENTIL AND SPINACH SOUP

Ingredients

- Lentils - 1 cup.
- Spinach, chopped - 2 cups.
- Onion, chopped - 1.
- Garlic cloves, minced - 2.
- Carrot, diced - 1.
- Tomato, chopped - 1.
- Vegetable broth - 6 cups.
- Cumin - 1 tsp.
- Salt - to taste.
- Black pepper - to taste.
- Lemon juice - 2 tbsp.
- Olive oil - 2 tbsp.

Instructions

1. In a large pot, heat the olive oil over medium heat. Add the onion, garlic, and carrot, cooking until the onion is soft.

2. Add the lentils, tomato, cumin, salt, and pepper, stirring to combine.

3. Pour in the vegetable broth and bring to a boil. Reduce heat to low and simmer until the lentils are almost done, about 20 minutes.

4. Add the spinach and cook until wilted, about 5 minutes.

5. Stir in the lemon juice and adjust the seasoning as needed.

6. Serve hot, optionally garnished with a drizzle of olive oil or lemon slices.

CARROT AND CORIANDER SOUP

Ingredients

- Carrots, peeled and chopped - 1 kg.
- Onion, chopped - 1.
- Vegetable stock - 5 cups.
- Ground coriander - 1 tsp.
- Fresh coriander, chopped - 2 tbsp.
- Olive oil - 2 tbsp.
- Salt - to taste.
- Black pepper - to taste.

Instructions

1. Heat the olive oil in a large pot over medium heat. Add the onion and cook until soft.

2. Add the carrots and ground coriander, stirring until the carrots are coated and the coriander is fragrant.

3. Pour in the vegetable stock and bring to a boil. Reduce the heat and simmer until the carrots are tender, about 20 minutes.

4. Use an immersion blender to puree the soup until smooth. Season with salt and pepper to taste.

5. Serve hot, garnished with fresh coriander.

SHORBAT ANBAR (AMBER SOUP)

Ingredients

- Lamb meat, cubed - 1 lb.
- Onion, finely chopped - 1.
- Rice, washed - 1/2 cup.
- Lemon juice - 3 tbsp.
- Parsley, chopped - 1/4 cup.
- Chicken stock - 6 cups.
- Salt - to taste.
- Black pepper - to taste.

Instructions

1. In a large pot, bring the chicken stock to a boil. Add the lamb and onion, reducing the heat to simmer until the lamb is nearly tender, about 1 hour.

2. Add the rice to the pot and continue to simmer until the rice is cooked, about 20 minutes.

3. Stir in the lemon juice, parsley, salt, and pepper. Cook for an additional 5 minutes.

4. Adjust the seasoning if necessary and serve hot.

BEETROOT SOUP

Ingredients

- Beetroots, peeled and diced - 3.

- Carrot, diced - 1.
- Onion, chopped - 1.
- Vegetable stock - 4 cups.
- Cumin - 1/2 tsp.
- Apple cider vinegar - 2 tbsp.
- Sour cream - for garnish.
- Salt - to taste.
- Black pepper - to taste.

Instructions

1. In a large pot, combine the beetroots, carrot, onion, and vegetable stock. Bring to a boil, then reduce heat and simmer until the vegetables are tender, about 30 minutes.

2. Stir in the cumin and apple cider vinegar.

3. Use an immersion blender to puree the soup until smooth. Season with salt and pepper to taste.

4. Serve hot, topped with a dollop of sour cream.

QUINOA AND VEGETABLE SOUP

Ingredients

- Quinoa, rinsed - 1 cup.
- Carrots, diced - 2.
- Zucchini, diced - 1.
- Onion, chopped - 1.
- Garlic cloves, minced - 2.
- Vegetable stock - 6 cups.
- Tomatoes, diced - 2.
- Cumin - 1 tsp.
- Olive oil - 2 tbsp.
- Salt - to taste.
- Black pepper - to taste.

Instructions

1. Heat the olive oil in a large pot over medium heat. Add the onion and garlic, cooking until the onion is soft.

2. Add the carrots, zucchini, cumin, salt, and pepper. Cook for a few minutes until the vegetables start to soften.

3. Stir in the quinoa and vegetable stock. Bring to a boil, then reduce the heat and simmer until the quinoa is cooked, about 15 minutes.

4. Add the tomatoes and simmer for an additional 5 minutes.

5. Adjust the seasoning if necessary and serve hot.

SHORBAT HULBA (FENUGREEK SOUP)

Ingredients

- Fenugreek seeds, soaked overnight - 1/4 cup.
- Lamb or chicken, cubed - 1 lb.
- Onion, chopped - 1.
- Garlic cloves, minced - 2.
- Tomato paste - 2 tbsp.
- Chicken stock - 6 cups.
- Lemon juice - 2 tbsp.
- Salt - to taste.
- Black pepper - to taste.
- Cilantro, chopped - for garnish.

Instructions

1. Drain and rinse the soaked fenugreek seeds. Blend them with a little water to make a paste.

2. In a large pot, cook the onion and garlic until soft. Add the meat and brown on all sides.

3. Stir in the tomato paste, fenugreek paste, chicken stock, salt, and pepper. Bring to a boil, then reduce heat and simmer until the meat is tender, about 1 hour.

4. Stir in the lemon juice just before serving.

5. Serve hot, garnished with chopped cilantro.

SALADS

Salads in Iraqi cuisine offer a refreshing counterpoint to the rich, hearty dishes that characterize the nation's culinary repertoire. They are a vibrant celebration of fresh produce, marrying textures and flavors in a way that is both satisfying and light. The diversity of salads reflects the agricultural bounty of Iraq, incorporating everything from leafy greens and ripe tomatoes to fragrant herbs and citrus, showcasing the versatility of ingredients available.

These dishes are not only prized for their taste but also for their health benefits, embodying the essence of a balanced diet. Iraqi salads are rich in vitamins, minerals, and fiber, thanks to the generous use of fresh vegetables, fruits, and wholesome grains. The judicious application of dressings, often made from olive oil and lemon juice, enhances flavors while adding beneficial fats, making these salads an integral part of a healthy eating plan.

Salads play a crucial role in Iraqi meals, acting as both palate cleansers and nutritional complements to the main dishes. Their simplicity and ease of preparation make them an indispensable part of daily dining, as well as festive gatherings, bridging the gap between tradition and health.

TABBOULEH

Ingredients

- Bulgur - 1/2 cup.
- Fresh parsley, finely chopped - 2 cups.
- Mint leaves, finely chopped - 1/4 cup.
- Tomatoes, finely diced - 3 medium.
- Cucumber, finely diced - 1 medium.
- Green onions, finely sliced - 3.

- Lemon juice - 1/4 cup.
- Extra virgin olive oil - 1/3 cup.
- Salt - to taste.
- Black pepper - to taste.

Instructions

1. Soak the bulgur in cold water for about 30 minutes until softened. Drain and squeeze out excess water.

2. In a large mixing bowl, combine the softened bulgur, parsley, mint, tomatoes, cucumber, and green onions.

3. In a small bowl, whisk together the lemon juice, olive oil, salt, and pepper. Pour over the salad and mix well.

4. Refrigerate for at least one hour to allow flavors to meld. Serve chilled.

FATTOUSH

Ingredients

- Romaine lettuce, chopped - 2 cups.
- Cucumber, diced - 1.
- Tomatoes, diced - 2.
- Radishes, thinly sliced - 4.
- Green onions, sliced - 2.
- Fresh mint, chopped - 1/4 cup.
- Pita bread, toasted and broken into pieces - 2.
- Sumac - 2 tsp.
- Lemon juice - 1/4 cup.
- Extra virgin olive oil - 1/3 cup.
- Salt - to taste.
- Black pepper - to taste.

Instructions

1. In a large salad bowl, combine the lettuce, cucumber, tomatoes, radishes, green onions, and mint.

2. Add the toasted pita pieces to the salad.

3. In a small bowl, whisk together the sumac, lemon juice, olive oil, salt, and pepper. Pour over the salad and toss well to combine.

4. Serve immediately to enjoy the crispy texture of the pita.

CUCUMBER YOGURT SALAD

Ingredients

- Cucumber, diced - 2 medium.
- Plain yogurt - 1 cup.
- Garlic, minced - 1 clove.
- Fresh dill, chopped - 2 tbsp.
- Lemon juice - 1 tbsp.
- Salt - to taste.
- Black pepper - to taste.

Instructions

1. In a mixing bowl, combine the cucumber, yogurt, garlic, dill, lemon juice, salt, and pepper.

2. Stir until well mixed.

3. Chill in the refrigerator for at least 30 minutes before serving to allow the flavors to blend.

4. Serve cold as a refreshing side dish.

TOMATO AND ONION SALAD

Ingredients

- Tomatoes, sliced - 3 large.
- Onion, thinly sliced - 1 large.
- Extra virgin olive oil - 2 tbsp.
- Lemon juice - 1 tbsp.
- Salt - to taste.
- Black pepper - to taste.
- Fresh parsley, chopped - 2 tbsp.

Instructions

1. In a salad bowl, layer the sliced tomatoes and onions.

2. In a small bowl, whisk together the olive oil, lemon juice, salt, and pepper.

3. Pour the dressing over the tomatoes and onions.

4. Garnish with chopped parsley.

5. Serve immediately or chill for a short time to enhance the flavors.

EGGPLANT SALAD

Ingredients

- Eggplants, roasted and peeled - 2 medium.
- Tomatoes, diced - 2.
- Green pepper, diced - 1.
- Onion, finely chopped - 1.
- Garlic, minced - 1 clove.
- Parsley, chopped - 1/4 cup.
- Lemon juice - 2 tbsp.

- Extra virgin olive oil - 3 tbsp.
- Salt - to taste.
- Black pepper - to taste.

Instructions

1. Cut the roasted eggplants into cubes and place them in a salad bowl.

2. Add the diced tomatoes, green pepper, onion, and garlic to the bowl.

3. Add the chopped parsley for freshness.

4. In a small bowl, mix together the lemon juice, olive oil, salt, and pepper to create the dressing.

5. Pour the dressing over the salad and gently toss to combine all the ingredients.

6. Serve chilled or at room temperature as a flavorful side dish.

BEETROOT SALAD

Ingredients

- Beetroots, cooked and sliced - 4 medium.
- Garlic, minced - 2 cloves.
- Extra virgin olive oil - 3 tbsp.
- Lemon juice - 2 tbsp.
- Salt - to taste.
- Black pepper - to taste.
- Fresh parsley, chopped - 1/4 cup.

Instructions

1. Place the sliced beetroots in a salad bowl.

2. Add the minced garlic and chopped parsley to the beets.

3. In a small bowl, whisk together the olive oil, lemon juice, salt, and pepper to create a dressing.

4. Pour the dressing over the beetroot mixture and toss gently to combine.

5. Chill in the refrigerator for at least 30 minutes before serving to allow the flavors to meld.

CARROT SALAD

Ingredients

- Carrots, grated - 4 large.
- Garlic, minced - 1 clove.
- Ground cumin - 1 tsp.
- Paprika - 1/2 tsp.
- Lemon juice - 2 tbsp.
- Extra virgin olive oil - 2 tbsp.
- Salt - to taste.
- Chopped parsley - 2 tbsp.

Instructions

1. In a large bowl, combine the grated carrots and minced garlic.

2. Sprinkle the ground cumin and paprika over the carrots.

3. Add the lemon juice, olive oil, and salt. Toss well to coat the carrots evenly with the dressing and spices.

4. Garnish with chopped parsley before serving.

5. Serve chilled or at room temperature as a refreshing side dish.

CHICKPEA SALAD

Ingredients

- Chickpeas, cooked - 2 cups.
- Tomatoes, diced - 2.
- Cucumber, diced - 1.
- Red onion, finely chopped - 1/2.
- Fresh parsley, chopped - 1/4 cup.
- Lemon juice - 3 tbsp.
- Extra virgin olive oil - 3 tbsp.
- Salt - to taste.
- Black pepper - to taste.

Instructions

1. In a large salad bowl, combine the chickpeas, diced tomatoes, diced cucumber, and chopped red onion.

2. Add the chopped parsley to the bowl.

3. In a small bowl, whisk together the lemon juice, olive oil, salt, and pepper to create a dressing.

4. Pour the dressing over the salad and toss gently to ensure all the ingredients are well coated.

5. Let the salad sit for at least 15 minutes before serving to allow the flavors to combine.

IRAQI POTATO SALAD

Ingredients

- Potatoes, boiled and cubed - 4 medium.
- Green onions, sliced - 2.
- Hard-boiled eggs, chopped - 2.
- Mayonnaise - 1/2 cup.
- Lemon juice - 1 tbsp.
- Salt - to taste.
- Black pepper - to taste.
- Fresh parsley, chopped - 1/4 cup.

Instructions

1. In a large bowl, mix together the cubed potatoes, sliced green onions, and chopped hard-boiled eggs.

2. In a separate bowl, combine the mayonnaise, lemon juice, salt, and pepper. Mix well to create the dressing.

3. Pour the dressing over the potato mixture and toss gently to coat everything evenly.

4. Garnish with chopped parsley before serving.

5. Chill in the refrigerator for at least 1 hour before serving to enhance the flavors.

GREEN BEAN SALAD

Ingredients

- Green beans, trimmed and blanched - 2 cups.
- Tomato, diced - 1.
- Red onion, thinly sliced - 1/2.
- Feta cheese, crumbled - 1/4 cup.

- Olive oil - 2 tbsp.
- Lemon juice - 1 tbsp.
- Salt - to taste.
- Black pepper - to taste.
- Fresh mint, chopped - 1 tbsp.

Instructions

1. In a salad bowl, combine the blanched green beans, diced tomato, and thinly sliced red onion.

2. Sprinkle the crumbled feta cheese over the salad.

3. In a small bowl, whisk together the olive oil, lemon juice, salt, and pepper to create a dressing.

4. Pour the dressing over the salad and toss gently to mix.

5. Garnish with chopped fresh mint before serving.

6. Serve chilled or at room temperature as a delicious side dish.

ROASTED PEPPER AND WALNUT SALAD

Ingredients

- Red bell peppers, roasted and peeled - 2.
- Walnuts, coarsely chopped - 1/2 cup.
- Garlic, minced - 1 clove.
- Pomegranate molasses - 2 tbsp.
- Extra virgin olive oil - 2 tbsp.
- Lemon juice - 1 tbsp.
- Salt - to taste.
- Black pepper - to taste.
- Fresh parsley, chopped - 2 tbsp.

Instructions

1. Cut the roasted peppers into strips and place them in a salad bowl.

2. Add the chopped walnuts and minced garlic to the bowl.

3. In a small bowl, whisk together the pomegranate molasses, olive oil, lemon juice, salt, and pepper to create a dressing.

4. Pour the dressing over the salad and toss gently to combine.

5. Garnish with chopped parsley before serving.

6. Serve at room temperature or chilled, as preferred.

RADISH AND PARSLEY SALAD

Ingredients

- Radishes, thinly sliced - 1 cup.
- Fresh parsley, chopped - 1/2 cup.
- Lemon juice - 2 tbsp.
- Extra virgin olive oil - 1 tbsp.
- Salt - to taste.
- Black pepper - to taste.

Instructions

1. In a salad bowl, combine the sliced radishes and chopped parsley.

2. In a small bowl, whisk together the lemon juice, olive oil, salt, and pepper to create a dressing.

3. Pour the dressing over the radish and parsley mixture and toss well to coat.

4. Serve immediately or let it sit for a few minutes to allow the flavors to meld.

SUMAC ONION SALAD

Ingredients

- Red onion, thinly sliced - 1.
- Sumac - 2 tsp.
- Lemon juice - 2 tbsp.
- Olive oil - 1 tbsp.
- Salt - to taste.
- Fresh parsley, chopped - 1 tbsp.

Instructions

1. Place the thinly sliced onion in a salad bowl.

2. Sprinkle the sumac over the onions and add the chopped parsley.

3. In a small bowl, mix together the lemon juice, olive oil, and salt to create a dressing.

4. Pour the dressing over the onions and toss well to combine.

5. Let the salad sit for about 10 minutes before serving to allow the flavors to blend.

POMEGRANATE AND SPINACH SALAD

Ingredients

- Spinach leaves, washed and dried - 4 cups.
- Pomegranate seeds - 1/2 cup.
- Walnuts, toasted and chopped - 1/4 cup.
- Feta cheese, crumbled - 1/4 cup.
- Extra virgin olive oil - 3 tbsp.
- Pomegranate molasses - 1 tbsp.
- Lemon juice - 1 tbsp.
- Salt - to taste.
- Black pepper - to taste.

Instructions

1. In a large salad bowl, combine the spinach leaves, pomegranate seeds, toasted walnuts, and crumbled feta cheese.

2. In a small bowl, whisk together the olive oil, pomegranate molasses, lemon juice, salt, and pepper to create a dressing.

3. Drizzle the dressing over the salad and toss gently to coat.

4. Serve immediately to ensure the spinach stays fresh and crisp.

MIXED PICKLE SALAD

Ingredients

- Mixed pickles, chopped - 2 cups.
- Tomatoes, diced - 1 cup.
- Cucumbers, diced - 1 cup.

- Red onion, thinly sliced - 1/2 cup.
- Fresh parsley, chopped - 1/4 cup.
- Extra virgin olive oil - 2 tbsp.
- Lemon juice - 1 tbsp.
- Salt - to taste.
- Black pepper - to taste.

Instructions

1. In a large salad bowl, combine the chopped mixed pickles, diced tomatoes, diced cucumbers, and thinly sliced red onion.

2. Add the chopped parsley to the salad mixture.

3. In a small bowl, mix together the olive oil, lemon juice, salt, and pepper to create a dressing.

4. Pour the dressing over the salad and toss well to ensure all ingredients are evenly coated.

5. Serve chilled as a refreshing side dish or appetizer.

RICE AND GRAINS

Rice and grains hold a place of honor in Iraqi cuisine, serving as the foundation for many iconic dishes that are central to the country's culinary identity. These staples are celebrated for their ability to absorb and complement the rich array of spices and flavors used in Iraqi cooking, from the aromatic basmati rice in biryani to the hearty bulgur in traditional salads. The versatility of rice and grains enables a vast spectrum of dishes, ranging from simple, comforting meals to elaborate festive platters, showcasing their integral role in both everyday and celebratory Iraqi dining.

Nutritionally, these grains are a powerhouse, providing essential energy, protein, and fiber that are vital for a balanced diet. They work in harmony with other ingredients, such as vegetables, legumes, and meats, to create meals that are both fulfilling and nutritious. The use of whole grains in particular, like bulgur and barley, adds depth to the cuisine while offering a range of health benefits, including supporting heart health and aiding digestion.

In the context of Iraqi meals, rice and grains are much more than just side dishes; they are a canvas for culinary expression and tradition. Their adaptability makes them perfectly suited to embody the flavors and nutritional ethos of Iraqi cuisine, making every meal a celebration of culture and well-being.

BIRYANI IRAQI

Ingredients

- Rice - 2 cups.
- Chicken, cut into pieces - 1 lb.

- Onions, thinly sliced - 2.
- Carrots, grated - 2.
- Raisins - 1/2 cup.
- Almonds, slivered - 1/4 cup.
- Garlic cloves, minced - 3.
- Curry powder - 2 tbsp.
- Cinnamon stick - 1.
- Bay leaves - 2.
- Cardamom pods - 4.
- Chicken broth - 4 cups.
- Salt - to taste.
- Vegetable oil - 3 tbsp.

Instructions

1. Rinse the rice under cold water until the water runs clear. Soak in water for 30 minutes, then drain.

2. In a large pot, heat the oil over medium heat. Add the onions, carrots, and garlic, cooking until they start to brown.

3. Add the chicken pieces, curry powder, cinnamon stick, bay leaves, and cardamom pods. Cook until the chicken is browned on all sides.

4. Pour in the chicken broth and bring to a boil. Add the rice, raisins, and almonds, stirring gently.

5. Reduce the heat to low, cover, and simmer until the rice is tender and the liquid is absorbed, about 20 minutes.

6. Remove from heat and let sit, covered, for 10 minutes before serving.

TIMMAN Z'AFFARAN (SAFFRON RICE)

Ingredients

- Rice - 2 cups.
- Water - 4 cups.
- Saffron threads - 1/4 tsp.
- Cardamom pods - 3.
- Salt - 1 tsp.
- Butter - 2 tbsp.

Instructions

1. Rinse the rice under cold water until the water runs clear. Soak in water for 30 minutes, then drain.

2. In a small bowl, soak the saffron threads in 2 tablespoons of hot water for 10 minutes.

3. In a large pot, bring the water to a boil. Add the soaked saffron (including the water), cardamom pods, salt, and butter.

4. Add the rice to the pot and return to a boil. Reduce heat to low, cover, and simmer for 20 minutes, or until the rice is tender and the liquid is absorbed.

5. Remove from heat and let sit, covered, for 5 minutes before serving.

DOLMA (STUFFED VEGETABLES WITH RICE)

Ingredients

- Bell peppers - 4.
- Zucchinis - 4.
- Tomatoes - 4.

- Rice, rinsed and drained - 1 cup.
- Ground lamb or beef - 1/2 lb.
- Onion, finely chopped - 1.
- Garlic cloves, minced - 2.
- Parsley, chopped - 1/4 cup.
- Mint, chopped - 2 tbsp.
- Pine nuts - 1/4 cup.
- Tomato paste - 2 tbsp.
- Chicken or vegetable broth - 2 cups.
- Salt - to taste.
- Black pepper - to taste.
- Allspice - 1 tsp.
- Lemon juice - 2 tbsp.
- Olive oil - 2 tbsp.

Instructions

1. Hollow out the bell peppers, zucchinis, and tomatoes, reserving the flesh.

2. In a bowl, mix the rice, ground meat, onion, garlic, parsley, mint, pine nuts, half of the tomato paste, salt, pepper, and allspice.

3. Stuff the hollowed vegetables with the rice mixture.

4. In a large pot, layer the reserved vegetable flesh at the bottom. Place the stuffed vegetables on top. Mix the remaining tomato paste with the broth, lemon juice, and olive oil, and pour over the stuffed vegetables.

5. Bring to a boil, then reduce heat to low, cover, and simmer for about 1 hour, or until the rice and vegetables are cooked through.

6. Serve the dolma warm, with the cooking broth drizzled on top if desired.

KABSA

Ingredients

- Rice - 2 cups.
- Chicken, cut into pieces - 1 lb.
- Onions, finely chopped - 2.
- Tomatoes, chopped - 3.
- Carrot, grated - 1.
- Garlic cloves, minced - 2.
- Kabsa spice mix - 2 tbsp.
- Bay leaves - 2.
- Cinnamon stick - 1.
- Chicken broth - 4 cups.
- Raisins - 1/2 cup.
- Almonds, toasted - 1/4 cup.
- Salt - to taste.
- Vegetable oil - 3 tbsp.

Instructions

1. In a large pot, heat the oil over medium heat. Add the onions and garlic, cooking until they begin to soften.

2. Add the chicken pieces and brown on all sides.

3. Stir in the tomatoes, carrot, kabsa spice mix, bay leaves, and cinnamon stick. Cook for a few minutes until fragrant.

4. Add the rice, chicken broth, and salt. Bring to a boil, then reduce heat to low, cover, and simmer for 20-25 minutes, or until the rice is cooked and the liquid is absorbed.

5. In the last 5 minutes of cooking, add the raisins. Garnish with toasted almonds before serving.

MAJBOOS

Ingredients

- Rice - 2 cups.
- Lamb or chicken, cut into pieces - 1 lb.
- Onions, sliced - 2.
- Tomatoes, chopped - 2.
- Garlic cloves, minced - 3.
- Ginger, minced - 2 tbsp.
- Baharat spice mix - 2 tbsp.
- Dried lime - 2.
- Chicken broth - 4 cups.
- Cilantro, chopped - 1/4 cup.
- Salt - to taste.
- Vegetable oil - 3 tbsp.

Instructions

1. In a large pot, heat the oil over medium heat. Add the onions, garlic, and ginger, cooking until the onions are translucent.

2. Add the lamb or chicken pieces and brown on all sides.

3. Stir in the tomatoes, baharat spice mix, dried lime, and salt. Cook for a few minutes until the tomatoes are softened.

4. Add the rice and chicken broth. Bring to a boil, then reduce heat to low, cover, and simmer for 20-25 minutes, or until the rice is cooked and the liquid is absorbed.

5. Stir in the chopped cilantro before serving.

QUZI (RICE WITH LAMB)

Ingredients

- Lamb shoulder - 2 lbs.
- Basmati rice - 2 cups.
- Onions, chopped - 2.
- Carrots, chopped - 2.
- Garlic cloves, minced - 4.
- Cardamom pods - 5.
- Cinnamon sticks - 2.
- Baharat spice mix - 2 tbsp.
- Salt - to taste.
- Black pepper - to taste.
- Vegetable oil - 3 tbsp.
- Water - 4 cups.
- Almonds, toasted - for garnish.
- Raisins - for garnish.

Instructions

1. In a large pot, heat the oil over medium heat. Add the lamb shoulder and brown on all sides. Remove and set aside.

2. In the same pot, add the onions, carrots, and garlic. Sauté until softened.

3. Return the lamb to the pot. Add the cardamom pods, cinnamon sticks, baharat, salt, and pepper. Cover with water and bring to a boil. Reduce heat to low, cover, and simmer until the lamb is tender, about 1.5 hours.

4. Rinse the rice until the water runs clear. Add to the pot with the lamb. Bring to a boil, then reduce heat to low, cover, and cook until the rice is tender and the liquid is absorbed, about 20 minutes.

5. Serve the quzi garnished with toasted almonds and raisins.

TIMMAN BAGILLA (RICE WITH FAVA BEANS)

Ingredients

- Basmati rice - 2 cups.
- Fava beans, canned or fresh - 1 cup.
- Onion, finely chopped - 1.
- Garlic cloves, minced - 2.
- Cumin - 1 tsp.
- Coriander - 1 tsp.
- Salt - to taste.
- Black pepper - to taste.
- Vegetable oil - 2 tbsp.
- Water - 3 cups.

Instructions

1. Rinse the rice under cold water until the water runs clear. Soak in water for 30 minutes, then drain.

2. In a pot, heat the oil over medium heat. Add the onion and garlic, and cook until soft and golden.

3. Stir in the fava beans, cumin, coriander, salt, and pepper. Cook for a few minutes to blend the flavors.

4. Add the rice and water to the pot. Bring to a boil, then reduce heat to low, cover, and simmer until the rice is tender and the liquid is absorbed, about 20 minutes.

5. Fluff the rice with a fork before serving.

HAREESA (WHEAT PORRIDGE WITH MEAT)

Ingredients

- Wheat berries - 1 cup.
- Lamb or chicken, cubed - 2 lbs.
- Onion, quartered - 1.
- Salt - to taste.
- Water - 6 cups.
- Butter - 2 tbsp.
- Cinnamon - for garnish.

Instructions

1. Soak wheat berries in water overnight, then drain.

2. In a large pot, combine the wheat berries, meat, onion, salt, and water. Bring to a boil, then reduce heat to low. Simmer, covered, stirring occasionally, until the meat is tender and the wheat berries are soft and the mixture is thick, about 2-3 hours.

3. Remove the onion and discard. Shred the meat into the mixture using a fork.

4. Stir in the butter until melted and combined.

5. Serve hot, garnished with cinnamon.

MASGOUF RICE

Ingredients

- Basmati rice - 2 cups.
- Tomatoes, diced - 2.
- Onion, finely chopped - 1.
- Garlic cloves, minced - 2.

- Turmeric - 1 tsp.
- Cumin - 1 tsp.
- Vegetable broth - 4 cups.
- Olive oil - 2 tbsp.
- Salt - to taste.
- Black pepper - to taste.

Instructions

1. Rinse the rice under cold water until the water runs clear. Soak in water for 30 minutes, then drain.

2. In a pot, heat the olive oil over medium heat. Add the onion and garlic, and sauté until golden.

3. Stir in the tomatoes, turmeric, cumin, salt, and pepper. Cook for a few minutes until the tomatoes are soft.

4. Add the rice and vegetable broth. Bring to a boil, then reduce heat to low, cover, and simmer until the rice is tender and the liquid is absorbed, about 20 minutes.

5. Fluff the rice with a fork before serving.

TASHREEB (BREAD SOAKED IN BROTH AND RICE)

Ingredients

- Basmati rice - 2 cups.
- Lamb or chicken broth - 4 cups.
- Arabic flatbread - 4 pieces.
- Lamb or chicken, cooked and shredded - 2 cups.
- Onions, sliced - 2.
- Tomatoes, chopped - 2.
- Garlic cloves, minced - 2.
- Turmeric - 1 tsp.

- Allspice - 1 tsp.
- Salt - to taste.
- Black pepper - to taste.
- Vegetable oil - 2 tbsp.
- Parsley, chopped - for garnish.

Instructions

1. Rinse the rice under cold water until the water runs clear. Soak in water for 30 minutes, then drain.

2. In a large pot, bring the broth to a boil. Add the rice, reduce heat to low, cover, and simmer until the rice is tender and the liquid is absorbed, about 20 minutes.

3. In another pan, heat the oil over medium heat. Sauté the onions and garlic until soft. Add the tomatoes, turmeric, allspice, salt, and pepper. Cook until the tomatoes are soft.

4. Break the flatbread into pieces and place at the bottom of a serving dish. Spoon the rice over the bread.

5. Top with the cooked meat and tomato-onion mixture.

6. Garnish with chopped parsley before serving.

MUTHALATHAT (TRIANGLE RICE)

Ingredients

- Basmati rice - 2 cups.
- Lamb meat, cubed - 1 lb.
- Carrots, diced - 2.
- Peas - 1 cup.
- Almonds, slivered - 1/4 cup.
- Raisins - 1/4 cup.

- Onion, finely chopped - 1.
- Garlic cloves, minced - 2.
- Cumin - 1 tsp.
- Cardamom - 1/2 tsp.
- Cinnamon stick - 1.
- Salt - to taste.
- Black pepper - to taste.
- Vegetable oil - 3 tbsp.
- Water - 4 cups.

Instructions

1. Rinse the rice under cold water until the water runs clear. Soak in water for 30 minutes, then drain.

2. In a large pot, heat the oil over medium heat. Add the lamb, onion, and garlic, cooking until the lamb is browned.

3. Add the carrots, peas, almonds, raisins, cumin, cardamom, cinnamon, salt, and pepper. Stir well to combine.

4. Add the rice and water to the pot. Bring to a boil, then reduce heat to low, cover, and simmer until the rice is cooked and the liquid is absorbed, about 20 minutes.

5. Let sit for 10 minutes before serving. Fluff with a fork and serve warm.

RICE WITH CHICKPEAS

Ingredients

- Basmati rice - 2 cups.
- Chickpeas, cooked - 1 cup.
- Onion, finely chopped - 1.

- Garlic cloves, minced - 2.
- Cumin - 1 tsp.
- Coriander - 1 tsp.
- Vegetable broth - 4 cups.
- Salt - to taste.
- Black pepper - to taste.
- Olive oil - 2 tbsp.

Instructions

1. Rinse the rice under cold water until the water runs clear. Soak in water for 30 minutes, then drain.

2. In a large pot, heat the olive oil over medium heat. Add the onion and garlic, and sauté until golden.

3. Add the chickpeas, cumin, coriander, salt, and pepper. Cook for a few minutes to blend the flavors.

4. Add the rice and vegetable broth. Bring to a boil, then reduce heat to low, cover, and simmer until the rice is tender and the liquid is absorbed, about 20 minutes.

5. Fluff the rice with a fork before serving. Serve warm.

RICE WITH DATES

Ingredients

- Basmati rice - 2 cups.
- Dates, pitted and chopped - 1 cup.
- Butter - 2 tbsp.
- Cardamom pods - 4.
- Cinnamon stick - 1.
- Salt - 1 tsp.
- Water - 4 cups.

Instructions

1. Rinse the rice under cold water until the water runs clear. Soak in water for 30 minutes, then drain.

2. In a pot, melt the butter over medium heat. Add the cardamom pods and cinnamon stick, and sauté for 1 minute.

3. Add the rice, dates, salt, and water to the pot. Bring to a boil, then reduce heat to low, cover, and simmer until the rice is tender and the liquid is absorbed, about 20 minutes.

4. Remove the cardamom pods and cinnamon stick. Fluff the rice with a fork and serve warm.

RICE WITH NUTS AND RAISINS

Ingredients

- Basmati rice - 2 cups.
- Raisins - 1/2 cup.
- Almonds, slivered - 1/2 cup.
- Pistachios, chopped - 1/4 cup.
- Butter - 3 tbsp.
- Cardamom pods - 5.
- Cinnamon stick - 1.
- Sugar - 2 tbsp.
- Salt - 1 tsp.
- Water - 4 cups.

Instructions

1. Rinse the rice under cold water until the water runs clear. Soak in water for 30 minutes, then drain.

2. In a pot, melt the butter over medium heat. Add the cardamom pods, cinnamon stick, almonds, pistachios, and raisins. Sauté for 2 minutes.

3. Add the rice, sugar, salt, and water to the pot. Bring to a boil, then reduce heat to low, cover, and simmer until the rice is tender and the liquid is absorbed, about 20 minutes.

4. Remove the cardamom pods and cinnamon stick. Fluff the rice with a fork and serve warm.

BARLEY PILAF

Ingredients

- Pearl barley - 1 cup.
- Onion, finely chopped - 1.
- Carrots, diced - 2.
- Mushrooms, sliced - 1 cup.
- Vegetable broth - 3 cups.
- Olive oil - 2 tbsp.
- Garlic cloves, minced - 2.
- Thyme - 1 tsp.
- Salt - to taste.
- Black pepper - to taste.

Instructions

1. Rinse the barley under cold water until the water runs clear.

2. In a large pot, heat the olive oil over medium heat. Add the onion, carrots, mushrooms, and garlic. Sauté until the vegetables are soft.

3. Add the barley, vegetable broth, thyme, salt, and pepper to the pot. Bring to a boil, then reduce heat to low, cover, and simmer until the barley is tender and the liquid is absorbed, about 45 minutes to 1 hour.

4. Fluff the barley with a fork before serving. Serve warm as a hearty side dish.

LAMB

Lamb is a cornerstone of Iraqi cuisine, revered for its tender texture and distinctive flavor that elevates a myriad of traditional dishes. It is intricately woven into the fabric of Iraqi culinary culture, serving as a symbol of hospitality and celebration. The versatility of lamb allows it to be prepared in countless ways, from slow-cooked stews and savory kebabs to richly spiced rice dishes, each method showcasing its ability to harmonize with a wide array of spices and ingredients.

Nutritionally, lamb is a valuable source of high-quality protein, essential vitamins, and minerals, contributing to a well-rounded diet. Its richness in iron and B vitamins makes it a crucial component of meals intended to nourish and satisfy. Furthermore, when prepared with traditional methods that emphasize balance and moderation, lamb dishes can be a part of a healthy eating lifestyle, providing both sustenance and pleasure.

In Iraqi cuisine, lamb is not just food; it's a tradition that brings families and communities together. Its presence on the table signifies a feast, making it an indispensable part of celebrations and everyday meals alike, embodying the essence of Iraqi hospitality and culinary artistry.

QUZI (ROASTED LAMB)

Ingredients

- Lamb shoulder - 4 lbs.
- Garlic cloves, minced - 4.
- Ground cumin - 2 tsp.
- Ground coriander - 2 tsp.
- Paprika - 1 tsp.

- Salt - 2 tsp.
- Black pepper - 1 tsp.
- Olive oil - 3 tbsp.
- Water - 1 cup.

Instructions

1. Preheat your oven to 325°F (165°C).

2. In a small bowl, mix together the minced garlic, cumin, coriander, paprika, salt, and black pepper.

3. Rub the lamb shoulder all over with the spice mixture.

4. Place the lamb in a roasting pan and drizzle with olive oil.

5. Add water to the bottom of the roasting pan. Cover tightly with foil.

6. Roast in the preheated oven for about 4 hours, or until the lamb is tender and falls off the bone.

7. Let the lamb rest for 10 minutes before carving. Serve with rice or your choice of sides.

KEBAB

Ingredients

- Ground lamb - 2 lbs.
- Onion, finely grated - 1.
- Garlic cloves, minced - 3.
- Parsley, finely chopped - 1/4 cup.
- Salt - 1 tsp.
- Black pepper - 1/2 tsp.
- Cumin - 1 tsp.

- Paprika - 1 tsp.
- Olive oil - for grilling.

Instructions

1. In a large bowl, combine the ground lamb, grated onion, minced garlic, chopped parsley, salt, black pepper, cumin, and paprika. Mix well.

2. Divide the mixture into equal portions and shape each portion around skewers to form kebabs.

3. Preheat the grill to medium-high heat and lightly oil the grate.

4. Grill the kebabs, turning occasionally, until browned and cooked through, about 10-12 minutes.

5. Serve hot with flatbread and your choice of dips or salads.

LAMB BIRYANI

Ingredients

- Basmati rice - 2 cups.
- Lamb, cut into pieces - 2 lbs.
- Onions, thinly sliced - 2.
- Tomatoes, chopped - 2.
- Ginger-garlic paste - 2 tbsp.
- Yogurt - 1 cup.
- Biryani masala - 2 tbsp.
- Saffron strands - a pinch.
- Milk - 1/4 cup.
- Salt - to taste.
- Oil - 3 tbsp.
- Water - 4 cups.

- Mint leaves - for garnish.

Instructions

1. Rinse the rice until water runs clear, soak for 30 minutes, then drain.

2. In a large pot, heat oil and fry the onions until golden brown. Remove half for garnishing.

3. Add the lamb to the pot with remaining onions, ginger-garlic paste, tomatoes, yogurt, biryani masala, and salt. Cook until lamb is tender.

4. In a separate pot, bring water to a boil, add the rice, and cook until it's 70% done. Drain the rice.

5. Layer the cooked lamb and partially cooked rice in a pot. Sprinkle saffron soaked in milk over the top.

6. Cover and cook on low heat for 20-25 minutes until the rice is fully cooked.

7. Garnish with fried onions and mint leaves. Serve hot.

LAMB DOLMA

Ingredients

- Grape leaves - 40 leaves.
- Ground lamb - 1 lb.
- Rice, rinsed and drained - 1 cup.
- Onion, finely chopped - 1.
- Parsley, chopped - 1/4 cup.
- Mint, chopped - 2 tbsp.
- Salt - 1 tsp.
- Black pepper - 1/2 tsp.

- Lemon juice - 2 tbsp.
- Vegetable broth - 2 cups.

Instructions

1. Blanch the grape leaves in boiling water for 2-3 minutes. Rinse under cold water and drain.

2. In a bowl, mix the ground lamb, rice, onion, parsley, mint, salt, and pepper.

3. Place a spoonful of the filling on each grape leaf and roll tightly, tucking in the sides.

4. Arrange the stuffed leaves in a pot, seam-side down. Pour over the lemon juice and vegetable broth.

5. Cover and simmer over low heat for about 1 hour, until the filling is cooked and the leaves are tender.

6. Serve warm with yogurt or lemon wedges.

LAMB KOFTA

Ingredients

- Ground lamb - 1 lb.
- Onion, finely chopped - 1 medium.
- Garlic cloves, minced - 2.
- Parsley, finely chopped - 1/4 cup.
- Cumin - 1 tsp.
- Coriander - 1 tsp.
- Paprika - 1 tsp.
- Salt - 1 tsp.
- Black pepper - 1/2 tsp.
- Olive oil - for brushing.

Instructions

1. In a large bowl, combine the ground lamb, onion, garlic, parsley, cumin, coriander, paprika, salt, and pepper. Mix well until the ingredients are evenly distributed.

2. Take a portion of the mixture and mold it around skewers to form elongated koftas. If you don't have skewers, you can also form them into patties.

3. Preheat the grill or a grill pan over medium-high heat. Brush the koftas with olive oil.

4. Place the koftas on the grill or grill pan. Cook for about 4-5 minutes on each side or until they are well browned and cooked through.

5. Serve the lamb koftas hot, accompanied by rice, salad, or pita bread, as desired.

LAMB SHANK STEW

Ingredients

- Lamb shanks - 4.
- Onions, chopped - 2.
- Garlic cloves, minced - 4.
- Carrots, chopped - 2.
- Potatoes, cubed - 3.
- Tomato paste - 2 tbsp.
- Beef or lamb broth - 4 cups.
- Bay leaves - 2.
- Cinnamon stick - 1.
- Salt - to taste.
- Black pepper - to taste.
- Olive oil - 2 tbsp.

Instructions

1. In a large pot, heat the olive oil over medium heat. Add the lamb shanks and brown on all sides. Remove and set aside.

2. In the same pot, add the onions and garlic, cooking until softened.

3. Stir in the tomato paste, then add the carrots, potatoes, broth, bay leaves, cinnamon stick, salt, and pepper.

4. Return the lamb shanks to the pot. Bring to a boil, then reduce heat to low, cover, and simmer for about 2 hours, or until the lamb is tender.

5. Adjust seasoning to taste and serve hot.

IRAQI LAMB CURRY

Ingredients

- Lamb, cubed - 2 lbs.
- Onions, chopped - 2.
- Garlic cloves, minced - 3.
- Ginger, grated - 2 tbsp.
- Curry powder - 3 tbsp.
- Tomatoes, chopped - 2.
- Chicken or lamb broth - 3 cups.
- Potatoes, cubed - 2.
- Carrots, sliced - 2.
- Salt - to taste.
- Pepper - to taste.
- Vegetable oil - 2 tbsp.

Instructions

1. Heat the oil in a large pot over medium heat. Add the onions, garlic, and ginger, cooking until the onions are translucent.

2. Add the lamb and curry powder, browning the lamb on all sides.

3. Stir in the tomatoes, broth, potatoes, and carrots. Season with salt and pepper.

4. Bring to a boil, then reduce heat to low, cover, and simmer for about 1 hour, or until the lamb is tender and the vegetables are cooked.

5. Adjust seasoning to taste and serve hot with rice or flatbread.

LAMB AND OKRA STEW

Ingredients

- Lamb, cubed - 1 lb.
- Okra, trimmed - 2 cups.
- Onion, chopped - 1.
- Garlic cloves, minced - 2.
- Tomato paste - 2 tbsp.
- Lamb or chicken broth - 4 cups.
- Lemon juice - 2 tbsp.
- Coriander, ground - 1 tsp.
- Salt - to taste.
- Black pepper - to taste.
- Olive oil - 2 tbsp.

Instructions

1. In a large pot, heat the olive oil over medium heat. Add the lamb and brown on all sides. Remove and set aside.

2. In the same pot, add the onion and garlic, cooking until the onion is soft.

3. Stir in the tomato paste, then add the okra, broth, lemon juice, coriander, salt, and pepper.

4. Return the lamb to the pot. Bring to a boil, then reduce heat to low, cover, and simmer for about 45 minutes, or until the lamb and okra are tender.

5. Adjust seasoning to taste and serve hot.

LAMB AND EGGPLANT STEW

Ingredients

- Lamb, cubed - 1 lb.
- Eggplants, cubed - 2.
- Onions, chopped - 2.
- Garlic cloves, minced - 3.
- Tomatoes, chopped - 3.
- Tomato paste - 1 tbsp.
- Chicken or lamb broth - 3 cups.
- Cinnamon stick - 1.
- Allspice - 1 tsp.
- Salt - to taste.
- Black pepper - to taste.
- Olive oil - 3 tbsp.

Instructions

1. Salt the eggplant cubes and let them sit for 30 minutes to draw out bitterness, then rinse and dry.

2. In a large pot, heat 2 tablespoons of olive oil over medium heat. Add the lamb and brown on all sides. Remove and set aside.

3. In the same pot, add the remaining oil, onions, and garlic, cooking until soft.

4. Add the eggplants, tomatoes, tomato paste, broth, cinnamon stick, allspice, salt, and pepper.

5. Return the lamb to the pot. Bring to a boil, then reduce heat to low, cover, and simmer for about 1 hour, or until the lamb and eggplants are tender.

6. Adjust seasoning to taste and serve hot with rice.

LAMB TIKKA

Ingredients

- Lamb leg, cut into cubes - 2 lbs.
- Yogurt - 1 cup.
- Garlic cloves, minced - 4.
- Ginger, grated - 2 tbsp.
- Paprika - 1 tsp.
- Cumin powder - 1 tsp.
- Coriander powder - 1 tsp.
- Turmeric - 1/2 tsp.
- Garam masala - 1 tsp.
- Lemon juice - 3 tbsp.
- Salt - to taste.
- Black pepper - to taste.

- Olive oil - for brushing.

Instructions

1. In a large bowl, mix together the yogurt, minced garlic, grated ginger, paprika, cumin, coriander, turmeric, garam masala, lemon juice, salt, and pepper to create the marinade.

2. Add the lamb cubes to the marinade, ensuring each piece is well coated. Cover and refrigerate for at least 4 hours, or overnight for best results.

3. Preheat your grill to medium-high heat. Thread the marinated lamb cubes onto skewers, leaving a small space between each piece.

4. Brush the grill with olive oil and place the skewers on the grill. Cook for about 10-12 minutes, turning occasionally, until the lamb is cooked to your desired level of doneness.

5. Serve the lamb tikka hot, garnished with slices of lemon and fresh cilantro, accompanied by flatbread or rice and a side of salad or yogurt sauce.

PACHA (STUFFED SHEEP'S STOMACH)

Ingredients

- Sheep's stomach - 1.
- Lamb meat, minced - 2 lbs.
- Rice, cooked - 1 cup.
- Onions, chopped - 2.
- Parsley, chopped - 1/2 cup.
- Allspice - 1 tsp.
- Salt - to taste.

- Black pepper - to taste.
- Water - for boiling.

Instructions

1. Clean the sheep's stomach thoroughly with cold water and salt, then rinse.

2. Mix the minced lamb, cooked rice, onions, parsley, allspice, salt, and pepper in a bowl.

3. Stuff the sheep's stomach with the mixture, then sew it closed securely.

4. In a large pot, place the stuffed stomach and cover with water. Bring to a boil, then reduce heat and simmer for about 2-3 hours, until fully cooked.

5. Remove from water, let cool slightly, then slice and serve.

LAMB AND POTATO STEW

Ingredients

- Lamb meat, cubed - 2 lbs.
- Potatoes, cubed - 3.
- Onions, chopped - 2.
- Garlic cloves, minced - 4.
- Tomato paste - 2 tbsp.
- Chicken or beef broth - 4 cups.
- Carrots, sliced - 2.
- Cumin - 1 tsp.
- Coriander - 1 tsp.
- Salt - to taste.
- Black pepper - to taste.
- Olive oil - 2 tbsp.

Instructions

1. In a large pot, heat the olive oil over medium heat. Add the lamb and brown on all sides.

2. Add the onions and garlic, cooking until softened.

3. Stir in the tomato paste, cumin, coriander, salt, and pepper. Cook for a few minutes.

4. Add the broth, potatoes, and carrots. Bring to a boil, then reduce heat and simmer until the lamb is tender and the vegetables are cooked, about 1-1.5 hours.

5. Adjust seasoning to taste and serve hot.

LAMB WITH GREEN BEANS

Ingredients

- Lamb meat, cubed - 2 lbs.
- Green beans, trimmed - 2 cups.
- Onions, sliced - 2.
- Garlic cloves, minced - 2.
- Tomatoes, diced - 2.
- Tomato paste - 1 tbsp.
- Water - 2 cups.
- Cumin - 1 tsp.
- Salt - to taste.
- Black pepper - to taste.
- Olive oil - 2 tbsp.

Instructions

1. In a large pot, heat the olive oil over medium heat. Add the lamb and brown on all sides.

2. Add the onions and garlic, cooking until the onions are translucent.

3. Stir in the tomatoes, tomato paste, cumin, salt, and pepper. Cook until the tomatoes are soft.

4. Add the green beans and water, cover, and simmer until the lamb is tender and the green beans are cooked, about 1 hour.

5. Serve hot, with rice or bread.

LAMB AND LENTIL SOUP

Ingredients

- Lamb meat, cubed - 1 lb.
- Red lentils - 1 cup.
- Onions, chopped - 1.
- Garlic cloves, minced - 2.
- Carrots, diced - 2.
- Cumin - 1 tsp.
- Chicken or beef broth - 6 cups.
- Tomato paste - 1 tbsp.
- Salt - to taste.
- Black pepper - to taste.
- Coriander leaves, chopped - for garnish.

Instructions

1. In a large pot, cook the lamb, onions, and garlic over medium heat until the lamb is browned.

2. Add the lentils, carrots, cumin, broth, tomato paste, salt, and pepper.

3. Bring to a boil, then reduce heat and simmer until the lentils and lamb are tender, about 1 hour.

4. Garnish with coriander leaves before serving.

PACHA (STUFFED SHEEP'S STOMACH)

Ingredients

- Sheep's stomach - 1.
- Lamb meat, minced - 1 lb.
- Rice, cooked - 1 cup.
- Onions, finely chopped - 2.
- Parsley, chopped - 1/4 cup.
- Allspice - 1 tsp.
- Salt - to taste.
- Black pepper - to taste.
- Water - for boiling.

Instructions

1. Clean the sheep's stomach thoroughly with cold water and salt, then rinse.

2. Mix the minced lamb, cooked rice, onions, parsley, allspice, salt, and pepper in a bowl.

3. Stuff the mixture into the sheep's stomach, then sew it closed securely.

4. Place the stuffed stomach in a large pot of boiling water. Simmer for about 2-3 hours, or until the meat is tender.

5. Remove from the pot, let cool slightly, then slice and serve.

LAMB AND POTATO STEW

Ingredients

- Lamb shoulder, cubed - 2 lbs.
- Potatoes, cubed - 3.
- Carrots, sliced - 2.
- Onions, chopped - 2.
- Garlic cloves, minced - 4.
- Tomato paste - 2 tbsp.
- Beef or lamb broth - 4 cups.
- Cumin - 1 tsp.
- Coriander - 1 tsp.
- Salt - to taste.
- Black pepper - to taste.
- Vegetable oil - 2 tbsp.

Instructions

1. In a large pot, heat the oil over medium heat. Add the lamb and brown on all sides. Remove and set aside.

2. In the same pot, add the onions and garlic. Cook until soft.

3. Return the lamb to the pot. Add the potatoes, carrots, tomato paste, broth, cumin, coriander, salt, and pepper.

4. Bring to a boil, then reduce heat and simmer, covered, for about 1 hour, or until the lamb and potatoes are tender.

5. Adjust seasoning if necessary and serve hot.

LAMB WITH GREEN BEANS

Ingredients

- Lamb meat, cubed - 1 lb.
- Green beans, trimmed - 2 cups.
- Onions, chopped - 1.
- Garlic cloves, minced - 2.
- Tomatoes, diced - 2.
- Tomato paste - 1 tbsp.
- Cumin - 1 tsp.
- Salt - to taste.
- Black pepper - to taste.
- Water - 2 cups.
- Olive oil - 2 tbsp.

Instructions

1. In a pot, heat the olive oil over medium heat. Add the onions and garlic, cooking until they are soft.

2. Add the lamb and brown on all sides.

3. Stir in the tomatoes, tomato paste, cumin, salt, and pepper. Cook for a few minutes until the tomatoes soften.

4. Add the green beans and water. Bring to a boil, then reduce heat, cover, and simmer for about 30 minutes, or until the lamb and beans are tender.

5. Adjust the seasoning to taste and serve hot.

LAMB AND LENTIL SOUP

Ingredients

- Lamb shank - 1 lb.
- Lentils - 1 cup.
- Onion, chopped - 1.
- Carrots, diced - 2.
- Garlic cloves, minced - 3.
- Cumin - 1 tsp.
- Coriander - 1 tsp.
- Chicken or beef broth - 6 cups.
- Salt - to taste.
- Black pepper - to taste.
- Bay leaves - 2.
- Lemon juice - 2 tbsp.

Instructions

1. Rinse the lentils and soak for about 30 minutes, then drain.

2. In a large pot, combine the lamb shank, onion, carrots, garlic, cumin, coriander, broth, salt, pepper, and bay leaves. Bring to a boil.

3. Reduce heat to low and simmer for about 1 hour, or until the lamb is tender.

4. Remove the lamb shank, shred the meat, and return it to the pot. Add the lentils and continue to simmer until the lentils are cooked, about 30 minutes.

5. Stir in the lemon juice before serving.

6. Serve hot, garnished with fresh parsley if desired.

LAMB SAMBUSAK

Ingredients

- For the dough:
- All-purpose flour - 3 cups.
- Warm water - 1 cup.
- Yeast - 1 tbsp.
- Sugar - 1 tsp.
- Salt - 1 tsp.
- Vegetable oil - 2 tbsp.
- For the filling:
- Ground lamb - 1 lb.
- Onion, finely chopped - 1.
- Pine nuts - 1/4 cup.
- Allspice - 1 tsp.
- Cinnamon - 1/2 tsp.
- Salt - to taste.
- Black pepper - to taste.

Instructions

1. For the dough, dissolve yeast and sugar in warm water. Let sit until frothy, about 10 minutes. In a large bowl, mix flour and salt. Add the yeast mixture and oil. Knead until smooth. Cover and let rise for 1 hour.

2. For the filling, heat a pan over medium heat. Cook the lamb and onions until browned. Add the pine nuts, allspice, cinnamon, salt, and pepper. Cook for an additional 5 minutes.

3. Preheat your oven to 375°F (190°C).

4. Divide the dough into small balls. Roll each out into a circle, place a spoonful of the lamb mixture in the center, then fold and seal the edges to form a half-moon shape.

5. Place the sambusak on a baking sheet. Bake for 20-25 minutes, or until golden brown.

6. Serve warm or at room temperature.

LAMB SHAWARMA

Ingredients

- Lamb leg, thinly sliced - 2 lbs.
- Yogurt - 1 cup.
- Lemon juice - 1/4 cup.
- Garlic cloves, minced - 4.
- Ground cumin - 2 tsp.
- Paprika - 2 tsp.
- Turmeric - 1 tsp.
- Cinnamon - 1/2 tsp.
- Cardamom - 1/2 tsp.
- Salt - to taste.
- Black pepper - to taste.
- Extra virgin olive oil - 2 tbsp.

Instructions

1. In a large bowl, combine yogurt, lemon juice, garlic, cumin, paprika, turmeric, cinnamon, cardamom, salt, pepper, and olive oil to create the marinade.

2. Add the lamb slices to the marinade, ensuring each piece is well coated. Cover and refrigerate for at least 4 hours, preferably overnight.

3. Preheat a grill or skillet over medium-high heat. Remove lamb from the marinade and cook for 3-4 minutes on each side or until cooked to your liking.

4. Serve the lamb shawarma with flatbread, fresh vegetables, and tahini sauce.

LAMB MASGOUF

Ingredients

- Whole lamb ribs - 3 lbs.
- Olive oil - 1/4 cup.
- Lemon juice - 1/4 cup.
- Garlic cloves, minced - 4.
- Salt - 2 tsp.
- Black pepper - 1 tsp.
- Ground cumin - 1 tsp.
- Sumac - 1 tsp.

Instructions

1. Preheat your grill to a medium-high heat.

2. In a small bowl, mix together olive oil, lemon juice, minced garlic, salt, pepper, cumin, and sumac to create a marinade.

3. Brush the lamb ribs generously with the marinade.

4. Place the lamb ribs on the grill and cook for about 10-15 minutes on each side or until they are well browned and cooked through.

5. Serve the lamb masgouf hot, garnished with fresh herbs and additional lemon slices on the side.

LAMB RIBS WITH RICE

Ingredients

- Lamb ribs - 2 lbs.
- Basmati rice - 2 cups.
- Onions, sliced - 2.
- Carrots, grated - 1.
- Garlic cloves, minced - 3.
- Bay leaves - 2.
- Cinnamon stick - 1.
- Cardamom pods - 5.
- Salt - to taste.
- Black pepper - to taste.
- Vegetable oil - 3 tbsp.
- Water - 4 cups.

Instructions

1. In a large pot, heat the oil over medium heat. Add the onions and garlic, cooking until they are soft and golden.

2. Add the lamb ribs, bay leaves, cinnamon stick, cardamom pods, salt, and pepper. Brown the ribs on all sides.

3. Add water to the pot and bring to a boil. Reduce heat, cover, and simmer for about 1 hour, or until the lamb is tender.

4. Rinse the rice under cold water until the water runs clear. Add the rice and grated carrots to the pot. Bring to a boil, then reduce heat to low, cover, and simmer until the rice is cooked and the liquid is absorbed, about 20 minutes.

5. Serve the lamb ribs over the rice, garnished with fresh herbs if desired.

STUFFED LAMB WITH RICE

Ingredients

- Lamb shoulder, deboned - 4 lbs.
- Basmati rice, cooked - 3 cups.
- Ground beef or lamb - 1 lb.
- Pine nuts - 1/2 cup.
- Raisins - 1/2 cup.
- Onions, finely chopped - 2.
- Allspice - 2 tsp.
- Cinnamon - 1 tsp.
- Nutmeg - 1/2 tsp.
- Salt - to taste.
- Black pepper - to taste.
- Butter - 2 tbsp.

Instructions

1. Preheat your oven to 350°F (175°C).

2. In a skillet, melt the butter and sauté the onions until translucent. Add the ground meat, pine nuts, raisins, allspice, cinnamon, nutmeg, salt, and pepper. Cook until the meat is browned.

3. Mix the cooked meat mixture with the cooked rice.

4. Stuff the lamb shoulder with the rice mixture, then sew the opening closed with kitchen twine.

5. Place the stuffed lamb in a roasting pan. Cover with foil and bake for about 2-3 hours, or until the lamb is tender.

6. Remove from oven and let rest for 15 minutes before slicing. Serve the stuffed lamb with additional rice if desired.

LAMB AND PEA STEW

Ingredients

- Lamb stew meat - 2 lbs.
- Frozen peas - 2 cups.
- Onions, chopped - 2.
- Garlic cloves, minced - 4.
- Tomato paste - 2 tbsp.
- Chicken or lamb broth - 4 cups.
- Bay leaves - 2.
- Thyme - 1 tsp.
- Salt - to taste.
- Black pepper - to taste.
- Vegetable oil - 2 tbsp.

Instructions

1. In a large pot, heat the oil over medium heat. Add the lamb meat and brown on all sides. Remove and set aside.

2. In the same pot, add the onions and garlic, cooking until they are soft.

3. Return the lamb to the pot. Add the tomato paste, broth, bay leaves, thyme, salt, and pepper. Bring to a boil, then reduce heat, cover, and simmer for about 1 hour, or until the lamb is tender.

4. Add the frozen peas and cook for an additional 10 minutes, or until the peas are cooked through.

5. Adjust the seasoning if necessary and serve hot.

BEEF

Beef occupies a special niche within Iraqi cuisine, offering a robust flavor profile that complements the rich tapestry of dishes unique to the region. It serves as a versatile protein, seamlessly integrating into a variety of culinary creations, from hearty stews and savory minced meat kebabs to richly layered casseroles. This adaptability showcases beef's ability to mingle with the myriad of spices and cooking techniques characteristic of Iraqi gastronomy, providing a canvas for the expression of both traditional and innovative recipes.

From a nutritional standpoint, beef is a powerhouse, packed with essential nutrients vital for health and well-being. It is a rich source of high-quality protein, iron, and B vitamins, which are crucial for maintaining energy levels, muscle health, and overall vitality. The inclusion of beef in a balanced diet, especially when paired with vegetables and whole grains, underscores its role in supporting a nutritious lifestyle, aligning with the principles of Iraqi culinary traditions that value both flavor and health.

In the realm of Iraqi cuisine, beef transcends its role as merely an ingredient; it embodies a tradition of communal dining and celebration. Its presence in a meal elevates the occasion, making it a cherished component of both everyday dining and festive gatherings, and reflecting the warmth and generosity inherent in Iraqi hospitality.

BEEF KEBAB

Ingredients

- Beef cubes - 500g.
- Olive oil - 2 tablespoons.

- Garlic, minced - 3 cloves.
- Lemon juice - 2 tablespoons.
- Salt - 1 teaspoon.
- Black pepper - 1/2 teaspoon.
- Onions, quartered - 2.
- Bell peppers, cut into pieces - 2.

Instructions

1. In a bowl, mix olive oil, garlic, lemon juice, salt, and black pepper.

2. Add beef cubes to the marinade and let sit for at least 2 hours or overnight in the refrigerator.

3. Thread the beef, onions, and bell peppers onto skewers.

4. Preheat grill to medium-high heat and grill kebabs, turning occasionally, until cooked to desired doneness.

BEEF BIRYANI

Ingredients

- Basmati rice - 2 cups.
- Beef, cut into cubes - 500g.
- Onions, thinly sliced - 2.
- Tomatoes, chopped - 2.
- Ginger-garlic paste - 1 tablespoon.
- Biryani masala - 2 tablespoons.
- Yogurt - 1/2 cup.
- Mint leaves, chopped - 1/4 cup.
- Saffron strands, soaked in 1/4 cup warm milk - a pinch.
- Salt - to taste.
- Oil - 3 tablespoons.

Instructions

1. Wash and soak basmati rice in water for 30 minutes. Drain and set aside.

2. In a large pot, heat oil and sauté onions until golden brown. Add ginger-garlic paste and sauté for another minute.

3. Add beef cubes and fry until they are browned on all sides.

4. Add tomatoes, biryani masala, yogurt, mint leaves, and salt. Cook until the beef is tender and the oil separates from the gravy.

5. In another pot, bring water to a boil, add the soaked and drained rice, and cook until it's 70% done. Drain the rice.

6. Layer the cooked beef and partially cooked rice in the pot. Sprinkle saffron milk over the top layer of rice.

7. Cover and cook on a low heat for 20-25 minutes or until the rice is fully cooked. Fluff and mix gently before serving.

KUBBEH (MEAT WITH BULGUR)

Ingredients

- Bulgur - 1 cup.
- Ground beef - 500g.
- Onion, finely chopped - 1.
- Allspice - 1 teaspoon.
- Salt - 1 teaspoon.
- Black pepper - 1/2 teaspoon.

- Pinch of cinnamon.
- Water - for soaking bulgur.

Instructions

1. Soak bulgur in water for 30 minutes, then drain thoroughly.

2. Mix the bulgur with half of the ground beef, onion, and spices until well combined.

3. Form the mixture into small balls or ovals.

4. Stuff each ball with the remaining ground beef, seasoned with salt, pepper, and a pinch of cinnamon.

5. Seal the balls and cook in boiling water or broth until they float to the surface and are cooked through.

STUFFED ZUCCHINI WITH BEEF

Ingredients

- Zucchini - 4, medium-sized.
- Ground beef - 400g.
- Rice, washed and drained - 1/2 cup.
- Tomato paste - 2 tablespoons.
- Garlic, minced - 2 cloves.
- Salt - 1 teaspoon.
- Black pepper - 1/2 teaspoon.
- Dried mint - 1 teaspoon.
- Water - as needed.

Instructions

1. Hollow out the zucchini, leaving a thick wall on the sides.

2. Mix ground beef, rice, tomato paste, garlic, salt, pepper, and dried mint in a bowl.

3. Stuff the zucchini with the beef mixture and place them in a pot.

4. Add enough water to cover the zucchini halfway. Bring to a boil, then simmer until the zucchini are tender and the rice is cooked.

BEEF AND TOMATO STEW

Ingredients

- Beef, cut into cubes - 500g.
- Onions, chopped - 2.
- Garlic, minced - 3 cloves.
- Tomatoes, chopped - 4.
- Tomato paste - 1 tablespoon.
- Beef broth - 2 cups.
- Carrots, sliced - 2.
- Potatoes, cubed - 2.
- Salt - to taste.
- Black pepper - to taste.
- Bay leaves - 2.

Instructions

1. In a large pot, sauté onions and garlic until soft.

2. Add beef and brown on all sides.

3. Add tomatoes and tomato paste, cook for a few minutes.

4. Add beef broth, carrots, potatoes, salt, pepper, and bay leaves.

5. Bring to a boil, then reduce heat and simmer until the beef is tender and the vegetables are cooked through.

IRAQI MEATBALLS

Ingredients

- Ground beef - 1 pound.
- Breadcrumbs - 1/2 cup.
- Egg - 1.
- Onion, finely chopped - 1.
- Garlic cloves, minced - 2.
- Cumin - 1 tsp.
- Salt - 1/2 tsp.
- Black pepper - 1/4 tsp.
- Parsley, chopped - 2 tbsp.

Instructions

1. Preheat your oven to 375°F (190°C).

2. In a large bowl, combine all the ingredients thoroughly.

3. Shape the mixture into balls and place them on a baking sheet.

4. Bake for 25-30 minutes, or until cooked through.

BEEF SHAWARMA

Ingredients

- Thinly sliced beef - 2 pounds.
- Yogurt - 1/2 cup.
- Lemon juice - 2 tbsp.
- Shawarma spice mix - 2 tbsp.
- Garlic cloves, minced - 3.

- Salt - to taste.
- Olive oil - 2 tbsp.

Instructions

1. In a bowl, mix together yogurt, lemon juice, shawarma spice, garlic, salt, and olive oil.

2. Add the beef slices to the marinade, ensuring they are well coated.

3. Cover and refrigerate for at least 2 hours, or overnight for best results.

4. Heat a grill or skillet over medium-high heat and cook the beef slices for 3-4 minutes on each side.

5. Serve hot with your choice of sides.

BEEF DOLMA

Ingredients

- Ground beef - 1 pound.
- Rice, rinsed and drained - 1 cup.
- Onion, finely chopped - 1.
- Tomato paste - 2 tbsp.
- Parsley, chopped - 1/4 cup.
- Mint, dried - 1 tsp.
- Salt - 1 tsp.
- Black pepper - 1/2 tsp.
- Grape leaves, rinsed and drained - 40 leaves.

Instructions

1. In a large bowl, mix together the ground beef, rice, onion, tomato paste, parsley, mint, salt, and pepper.

2. Place a spoonful of the mixture in the center of a grape leaf and roll it tightly.

3. Repeat with the remaining leaves and filling.

4. Arrange the stuffed leaves in a pot, cover with water, and bring to a boil.

5. Reduce the heat and simmer for about 1 hour, until the rice and meat are cooked.

BAKED KOFTA WITH POTATOES

Ingredients

- Ground beef - 1 pound.
- Onion, grated - 1.
- Garlic cloves, minced - 2.
- Parsley, chopped - 1/4 cup.
- Cumin - 1 tsp.
- Salt - 1 tsp.
- Black pepper - 1/2 tsp.
- Potatoes, sliced - 4.
- Tomatoes, sliced - 2.

Instructions

1. Preheat your oven to 400°F (200°C).

2. In a bowl, mix together ground beef, onion, garlic, parsley, cumin, salt, and pepper.

3. Shape the mixture into elongated koftas.

4. In a baking dish, layer the potato slices, then place the koftas on top, and cover with tomato slices.

5. Bake for 40-45 minutes, until the meat is cooked and potatoes are tender.

BEEF SAMOON SANDWICH

Ingredients

- Thinly sliced roast beef - 1 pound.
- Samoon bread - 4 pieces.
- Mayonnaise - 1/4 cup.
- Mustard - 2 tbsp.
- Lettuce leaves - 4.
- Tomato, sliced - 1.
- Onion, sliced - 1.
- Pickle slices - 8.

Instructions

1. Spread mayonnaise and mustard on the inside of each piece of bread.

2. Layer the roast beef, lettuce, tomato, onion, and pickles on the bread.

3. Close the sandwiches and serve immediately.

BEEF AND SPINACH STEW

Ingredients

- Beef stew meat, cubed - 1 pound.
- Spinach, washed and chopped - 1 pound.
- Onion, chopped - 1.
- Garlic cloves, minced - 2.
- Tomato paste - 2 tbsp.
- Beef broth - 4 cups.
- Cumin - 1 tsp.

- Salt - to taste.
- Black pepper - to taste.

Instructions

1. In a large pot, sauté the onion and garlic until translucent.

2. Add the beef and brown on all sides.

3. Stir in the tomato paste, beef broth, cumin, salt, and pepper.

4. Bring to a boil, then reduce the heat and simmer for about 1 hour, until the beef is tender.

5. Add the spinach and cook for an additional 10 minutes.

BEEF AND CHICKPEA STEW

Ingredients

- Beef cubes - 500g.
- Chickpeas, soaked overnight - 1 cup.
- Onion, chopped - 1 large.
- Garlic cloves, minced - 2.
- Tomato paste - 2 tablespoons.
- Carrots, diced - 2.
- Potatoes, cubed - 2.
- Cumin powder - 1 teaspoon.
- Coriander powder - 1 teaspoon.
- Beef stock - 4 cups.
- Salt and pepper - To taste.

Instructions

1. In a large pot, brown the beef cubes over medium heat and set aside.

2. In the same pot, sauté the onion and garlic until translucent.

3. Add the tomato paste, cumin, and coriander powder, cooking for another 2 minutes.

4. Return the beef to the pot, add the chickpeas, carrots, potatoes, beef stock, salt, and pepper.

5. Bring to a boil, then reduce the heat and simmer for 1-1.5 hours, or until the beef is tender and the stew has thickened.

BEEF SAMBUSAK

Ingredients

- Ground beef - 500g.
- Onion, finely chopped - 1.
- Pine nuts - 1/4 cup.
- All-purpose flour - 2 cups.
- Water - as needed.
- Olive oil - 1 tablespoon.
- Salt and pepper - To taste.
- Cumin powder - 1/2 teaspoon.

Instructions

1. Prepare the dough by mixing flour, water, a pinch of salt, and olive oil until a soft dough forms. Let it rest for 30 minutes.

2. For the filling, sauté the onions in a pan until translucent, add the ground beef, pine nuts, salt, pepper, and cumin, and cook until the beef is browned.

3. Roll out the dough and cut into circles. Place a spoonful of the beef mixture in the center of each circle.

4. Fold the dough over the filling to create a half-moon shape and press the edges to seal.

5. Fry the sambusak in hot oil until golden brown.

BEEF STUFFED BREAD

Ingredients

- Ground beef - 400g.
- Bread dough - 500g (pre-made or homemade).
- Onion, chopped - 1.
- Tomato, chopped - 1.
- Green bell pepper, chopped - 1.
- Garlic cloves, minced - 2.
- Paprika - 1 teaspoon.
- Black olives, sliced - 1/4 cup.
- Salt and pepper - To taste.
- Cheddar cheese, shredded - 1/2 cup.

Instructions

1. Preheat the oven to 180°C (356°F).

2. In a pan, cook the ground beef with onions, garlic, tomato, green bell pepper, paprika, salt, and pepper until fully cooked.

3. Roll out the bread dough on a floured surface and spread the beef mixture evenly on top.

4. Sprinkle with black olives and cheddar cheese.

5. Roll the dough over the filling to create a log shape, sealing the edges.

6. Bake for 25-30 minutes, or until the bread is golden brown.

BEEF AND BARLEY SOUP

Ingredients

- Beef stew meat, cut into cubes - 500g.
- Barley, rinsed - 1 cup.
- Carrots, diced - 2.
- Celery stalks, diced - 2.
- Onion, chopped - 1.
- Garlic cloves, minced - 2.
- Beef broth - 6 cups.
- Bay leaf - 1.
- Thyme - 1 teaspoon.
- Salt and pepper - To taste.

Instructions

1. In a large pot, brown the beef cubes over medium-high heat.

2. Add the onions and garlic, cooking until softened.

3. Add the beef broth, barley, carrots, celery, bay leaf, thyme, salt, and pepper.

4. Bring to a boil, then reduce the heat, cover, and simmer for about 1 hour or until the barley and beef are tender.

BEEF CURRY WITH VEGETABLES

Ingredients

- Beef cubes - 500g.
- Coconut milk - 400ml.
- Carrots, sliced - 2.
- Potatoes, cubed - 2.
- Onion, chopped - 1.
- Garlic cloves, minced - 2.
- Curry powder - 2 tablespoons.
- Chili powder - 1 teaspoon (optional).
- Vegetable oil - 2 tablespoons.
- Salt and pepper - To taste.

Instructions

1. Heat the oil in a large pot, add the onion and garlic, and sauté until translucent.

2. Add the beef and cook until browned on all sides.

3. Stir in the curry powder (and chili powder if using), cooking for another minute.

4. Add the coconut milk, carrots, and potatoes. Season with salt and pepper.

5. Bring to a boil, then reduce the heat and simmer for about 30 minutes, or until the vegetables are tender and the beef is cooked through.

MEAT STUFFED ONIONS

Ingredients

- Large onions - 4.
- Ground beef - 500g.
- Rice, cooked - 1 cup.
- Pine nuts - 1/4 cup.
- Allspice - 1 teaspoon.
- Cinnamon - 1/2 teaspoon.
- Salt and pepper - To taste.

Instructions

1. Cut the top and bottom off each onion and remove the outer skin. Carefully separate the layers.

2. Mix the ground beef, cooked rice, pine nuts, allspice, cinnamon, salt, and pepper in a bowl.

3. Place a spoonful of the meat mixture on each onion layer, roll it up, and place in a baking dish.

4. Cover with tomato sauce and bake in a preheated oven at 180°C (356°F) for about 45 minutes or until the meat is cooked through.

BEEF AND RICE CASSEROLE

Ingredients

- Ground beef - 500g.
- White rice, uncooked - 1 cup.
- Onion, diced - 1.
- Garlic cloves, minced - 2.
- Tomato sauce - 2 cups.
- Chicken broth - 2 cups.

- Mixed vegetables (carrots, peas, corn) - 1 cup.
- Salt and pepper - To taste.

Instructions

1. In a skillet over medium heat, cook the ground beef with onion and garlic until browned.

2. Stir in the uncooked rice, tomato sauce, chicken broth, mixed vegetables, salt, and pepper.

3. Transfer to a casserole dish and bake in a preheated oven at 180°C (356°F) for about 60 minutes or until the rice is tender.

BEEF AND PUMPKIN STEW

Ingredients

- Beef cubes - 500g.
- Pumpkin, cubed - 2 cups.
- Onion, chopped - 1.
- Garlic cloves, minced - 2.
- Beef broth - 4 cups.
- Tomato paste - 1 tablespoon.
- Cumin - 1 teaspoon.
- Cinnamon - 1/2 teaspoon.
- Salt and pepper - To taste.

Instructions

1. In a large pot, brown the beef cubes, then remove and set aside.

2. In the same pot, sauté the onion and garlic until translucent.

3. Add the pumpkin, beef, beef broth, tomato paste, cumin, cinnamon, salt, and pepper.

4. Bring to a boil, then reduce heat and simmer for about 1 hour or until the beef and pumpkin are tender.

BEEF MASGOUF

Ingredients

- Beef fillets - 500g.
- Olive oil - 2 tablespoons.
- Lemon juice - 2 tablespoons.
- Garlic cloves, minced - 2.
- Ground cumin - 1 teaspoon.
- Ground coriander - 1 teaspoon.
- Salt and pepper - To taste.
- Tomatoes, sliced - 2.
- Onions, sliced - 2.

Instructions

1. Marinate the beef fillets in olive oil, lemon juice, garlic, cumin, coriander, salt, and pepper for at least 2 hours.

2. Place the beef fillets on a baking sheet, and arrange the tomato and onion slices on top.

3. Grill under a preheated grill or barbecue for about 10-15 minutes on each side or until the beef is cooked to your liking.

CHICKEN

Chicken is a pivotal element in Iraqi cuisine, celebrated for its delicate flavor and the way it absorbs the rich blend of spices and herbs traditional to the region. It is a versatile protein that finds its way into a plethora of dishes, from aromatic biryanis and succulent grilled kebabs to comforting soups and stews. This adaptability allows chicken to be a canvas for culinary creativity, bridging the gap between the simplicity of home cooking and the complexity of festive feasts, making it a beloved choice across all dining contexts.

Nutritionally, chicken stands out for its lean protein, offering a healthier alternative to red meats while still providing a satisfying base for meals. It's rich in essential nutrients like vitamins B6 and B12, niacin, and selenium, which support energy metabolism and overall health. The incorporation of chicken into Iraqi dishes contributes to a balanced diet, aligning with dietary recommendations for a healthy lifestyle without sacrificing taste or cultural authenticity.

In the landscape of Iraqi cuisine, chicken is more than just an ingredient; it represents a blend of tradition and nutrition. Its widespread use in everyday meals and special occasions alike underscores its integral role in promoting communal dining and wholesome eating, epitomizing the spirit of Iraqi hospitality and culinary heritage.

CHICKEN BIRYANI

Ingredients

- Chicken pieces - 1kg.
- Basmati rice - 2 cups.

- Onion, sliced - 1 large.
- Tomatoes, chopped - 2.
- Yogurt - 1 cup.
- Ginger-garlic paste - 2 tablespoons.
- Biryani masala - 2 tablespoons.
- Turmeric powder - 1 teaspoon.
- Saffron strands - a pinch.
- Milk - 2 tablespoons.
- Salt - to taste.
- Oil - for cooking.
- Water - as needed.
- Cilantro, chopped - for garnish.
- Mint leaves - for garnish.

Instructions

1. Marinate the chicken pieces with yogurt, biryani masala, turmeric powder, and ginger-garlic paste for at least 2 hours.

2. Soak the basmati rice in water for 30 minutes, then drain.

3. In a large pot, heat oil and fry the onions until golden brown. Remove half for garnishing.

4. Add the marinated chicken to the pot and cook until the chicken is half done.

5. Add tomatoes and cook until they soften.

6. Layer the soaked rice over the chicken. Mix saffron in milk and pour it over the rice.

7. Cover and cook on low heat until the rice is done and the chicken is tender.

8. Garnish with fried onions, cilantro, and mint leaves. Serve hot.

CHICKEN KEBAB

Ingredients

- Chicken breast, cubed - 500g.
- Yogurt - 1/2 cup.
- Lemon juice - 2 tablespoons.
- Garlic cloves, minced - 3.
- Paprika - 1 teaspoon.
- Cumin powder - 1 teaspoon.
- Salt - to taste.
- Pepper - to taste.
- Vegetable oil - 2 tablespoons.
- Skewers - as needed.

Instructions

1. In a bowl, mix together yogurt, lemon juice, minced garlic, paprika, cumin, salt, pepper, and vegetable oil to make the marinade.

2. Add the chicken cubes to the marinade and let it marinate for at least 2 hours, or overnight for best results.

3. Thread the marinated chicken cubes onto skewers.

4. Preheat the grill to medium-high heat and cook the skewers, turning occasionally, until the chicken is golden brown and cooked through.

5. Serve hot with your choice of side.

CHICKEN SHAWARMA

Ingredients

- Chicken thighs, boneless - 1kg.
- Yogurt - 1 cup.
- Lemon juice - 3 tablespoons.
- Shawarma spice mix - 2 tablespoons.
- Garlic cloves, crushed - 4.
- Salt - to taste.
- Olive oil - 2 tablespoons.
- Pita bread - for serving.
- Tahini sauce - for serving.
- Cucumber, sliced - for garnish.
- Tomato, sliced - for garnish.
- Onion, sliced - for garnish.

Instructions

1. Combine yogurt, lemon juice, shawarma spice mix, crushed garlic, salt, and olive oil in a bowl to prepare the marinade.

2. Add chicken thighs to the marinade, ensuring each piece is well-coated. Marinate for at least 4 hours or overnight.

3. Preheat your grill or skillet over medium heat, and cook the chicken until it is browned on all sides and fully cooked.

4. Slice the cooked chicken thinly.

5. Serve the chicken wrapped in pita bread, topped with tahini sauce, cucumber, tomato, and onion slices.

TASHREEB DAJAJ
(CHICKEN AND BREAD STEW)

Ingredients

- Chicken pieces - 1kg.
- Arabic flatbread, torn into pieces - 3.
- Onion, chopped - 1 large.
- Tomato, chopped - 2.
- Garlic cloves, minced - 3.
- Chicken stock - 4 cups.
- Turmeric powder - 1 teaspoon.
- Allspice - 1/2 teaspoon.
- Salt - to taste.
- Pepper - to taste.
- Cilantro, chopped - for garnish.

Instructions

1. In a large pot, cook the chicken pieces with onions, garlic, salt, and pepper until the chicken is browned.

2. Add tomatoes, turmeric, and allspice, and cook for a few minutes until the tomatoes soften.

3. Add chicken stock and bring to a boil. Reduce the heat and simmer until the chicken is tender.

4. Place the torn pieces of bread in a serving dish and pour the chicken stew over it.

5. Garnish with chopped cilantro and serve warm.

CHICKEN AND RICE SOUP

Ingredients

- Chicken breast, diced - 500g.
- Rice, washed - 1 cup.
- Carrot, diced - 1.
- Celery stalk, diced - 1.
- Onion, chopped - 1.
- Garlic cloves, minced - 2.
- Chicken broth - 6 cups.
- Salt - to taste.
- Pepper - to taste.
- Lemon juice - 2 tablespoons.
- Parsley, chopped - for garnish.

Instructions

1. In a large pot, bring the chicken broth to a boil. Add the diced chicken, rice, carrot, celery, onion, and garlic.

2. Season with salt and pepper to taste.

3. Reduce the heat and simmer for about 20-25 minutes, or until the rice and chicken are cooked through.

4. Stir in the lemon juice just before serving.

5. Garnish with chopped parsley and serve hot.

CHICKEN DOLMA

Ingredients

- Chicken breast, minced - 500g.
- Grape leaves - 40 leaves.
- Rice, washed and drained - 1 cup.

- Onion, finely chopped - 1 large.
- Tomato paste - 2 tablespoons.
- Parsley, chopped - 1/2 cup.
- Mint, dried - 1 tablespoon.
- Sumac - 1 teaspoon.
- Salt - to taste.
- Pepper - to taste.
- Lemon juice - 2 tablespoons.
- Olive oil - for cooking.

Instructions

1. Mix the minced chicken with rice, onion, parsley, mint, sumac, salt, pepper, and lemon juice.

2. Blanch grape leaves in boiling water for a few seconds, then drain.

3. Place a spoonful of the chicken mixture on each grape leaf and roll tightly.

4. Arrange the dolmas in a pot, pour over olive oil and enough water to cover, and simmer for about 1 hour or until cooked through.

5. Serve hot with a side of yogurt.

IRAQI CHICKEN CURRY

Ingredients

- Chicken pieces - 1kg.
- Onions, sliced - 2.
- Garlic cloves, minced - 3.
- Ginger, grated - 1 tablespoon.
- Tomatoes, chopped - 3.
- Curry powder - 2 tablespoons.

- Turmeric powder - 1 teaspoon.
- Chicken broth - 4 cups.
- Potatoes, cubed - 2.
- Carrots, sliced - 2.
- Salt - to taste.
- Pepper - to taste.
- Cilantro, chopped - for garnish.

Instructions

1. In a large pot, sauté onions, garlic, and ginger until golden.

2. Add chicken pieces and brown on all sides.

3. Stir in tomatoes, curry powder, and turmeric, cooking until fragrant.

4. Pour in chicken broth, add potatoes and carrots, and season with salt and pepper.

5. Simmer until chicken is cooked through and vegetables are tender.

6. Garnish with cilantro and serve with rice or flatbread.

CHICKEN AND VEGETABLE STEW

Ingredients

- Chicken thighs - 6.
- Onion, chopped - 1.
- Garlic cloves, minced - 3.
- Potatoes, cubed - 3.
- Carrots, sliced - 2.
- Zucchini, sliced - 2.
- Tomato paste - 2 tablespoons.

- Chicken broth - 4 cups.
- Bay leaves - 2.
- Salt - to taste.
- Pepper - to taste.

Instructions

1. In a large pot, brown the chicken thighs on both sides, then remove and set aside.

2. In the same pot, sauté onion and garlic until soft.

3. Add potatoes, carrots, zucchini, tomato paste, chicken broth, bay leaves, salt, and pepper.

4. Return the chicken to the pot, bring to a boil, then simmer until the chicken is cooked and vegetables are tender.

5. Adjust seasoning and serve hot.

CHICKEN KUBBEH

Ingredients

- Bulgur wheat - 2 cups.
- Chicken breast, minced - 500g.
- Onion, finely chopped - 1.
- Allspice - 1 teaspoon.
- Salt - to taste.
- Pepper - to taste.
- Oil - for frying.

Instructions

1. Soak bulgur wheat in water for 30 minutes, then drain well.

2. Mix bulgur with minced chicken, onion, allspice, salt, and pepper until well combined.

3. Form the mixture into small balls or ovals.

4. Fry in hot oil until golden and cooked through.

5. Serve with a side of yogurt or tahini sauce.

CHICKEN MASGOUF

Ingredients

- Whole chicken, split open - 1.
- Garlic cloves, crushed - 4.
- Lemon juice - 3 tablespoons.
- Olive oil - 2 tablespoons.
- Salt - to taste.
- Pepper - to taste.
- Curry powder - 1 tablespoon.
- Sumac - 1 teaspoon.

Instructions

1. Preheat your grill to medium-high heat.

2. Mix garlic, lemon juice, olive oil, salt, pepper, curry powder, and sumac in a bowl to make the marinade.

3. Rub the marinade all over the chicken and inside it.

4. Place the chicken on the grill, skin-side down, and cook for about 10-15 minutes on each side or until fully cooked and crispy.

5. Serve hot, garnished with lemon wedges and fresh herbs.

ROASTED CHICKEN WITH SAFFRON RICE

Ingredients

- Whole chicken - 1.5kg.
- Saffron strands - a pinch.
- Basmati rice - 2 cups.
- Chicken broth - 4 cups.
- Onion, finely chopped - 1.
- Garlic cloves, minced - 3.
- Salt - to taste.
- Pepper - to taste.
- Olive oil - 2 tablespoons.
- Almonds, slivered - for garnish.
- Parsley, chopped - for garnish.

Instructions

1. Preheat the oven to 200°C (392°F). Season the chicken with salt, pepper, and olive oil.

2. Roast the chicken in the oven for 1-1.5 hours, or until fully cooked and golden brown.

3. While the chicken is roasting, soak the saffron in 2 tablespoons of hot water for 10 minutes.

4. In a pot, sauté the onion and garlic in olive oil until translucent. Add the rice and saffron water, stirring for 2 minutes.

5. Add the chicken broth and bring to a boil. Reduce heat, cover, and simmer for 20 minutes, or until the rice is cooked.

6. Serve the roasted chicken over the saffron rice, garnished with almonds and parsley.

CHICKEN AND POTATO STEW

Ingredients

- Chicken pieces - 1kg.
- Potatoes, cubed - 3.
- Onion, chopped - 1.
- Garlic cloves, minced - 2.
- Tomato paste - 2 tablespoons.
- Chicken broth - 4 cups.
- Bay leaves - 2.
- Cumin powder - 1 teaspoon.
- Salt - to taste.
- Pepper - to taste.
- Olive oil - 2 tablespoons.

Instructions

1. In a large pot, heat the olive oil and brown the chicken pieces. Remove and set aside.

2. In the same pot, sauté the onion and garlic until soft.

3. Add the tomato paste, cumin, salt, and pepper, stirring for 2 minutes.

4. Return the chicken to the pot, add the potatoes, chicken broth, and bay leaves.

5. Bring to a boil, then reduce heat, cover, and simmer for 40 minutes, or until the chicken and potatoes are tender.

CHICKEN WITH OKRA

Ingredients

- Chicken pieces - 1kg.

- Okra, trimmed - 500g.
- Onion, chopped - 1.
- Garlic cloves, minced - 2.
- Tomato paste - 1 tablespoon.
- Tomatoes, diced - 2.
- Lemon juice - 2 tablespoons.
- Chicken broth - 3 cups.
- Cumin powder - 1 teaspoon.
- Coriander powder - 1 teaspoon.
- Salt - to taste.
- Pepper - to taste.
- Olive oil - 2 tablespoons.

Instructions

1. In a large pot, sauté the onion and garlic in olive oil until soft.

2. Add the chicken pieces and brown on all sides.

3. Stir in the tomato paste, diced tomatoes, cumin, coriander, salt, and pepper. Cook for 5 minutes.

4. Add the okra, chicken broth, and lemon juice. Bring to a boil, then reduce heat and simmer for 30 minutes.

CHICKEN WITH POMEGRANATE MOLASSES

Ingredients

- Chicken thighs, bone-in - 8.
- Pomegranate molasses - 1/4 cup.
- Garlic cloves, minced - 3.
- Olive oil - 2 tablespoons.
- Thyme - 1 teaspoon.
- Salt - to taste.
- Pepper - to taste.

- Walnuts, crushed - for garnish.
- Pomegranate seeds - for garnish.

Instructions

1. Preheat the oven to 200°C (392°F).

2. In a bowl, mix the pomegranate molasses, garlic, olive oil, thyme, salt, and pepper.

3. Coat the chicken thighs in the mixture and place in a baking dish.

4. Roast for 35-40 minutes, or until the chicken is cooked through and the skin is crispy.

5. Garnish with crushed walnuts and pomegranate seeds before serving.

SUMAC CHICKEN

Ingredients

- Chicken breasts - 4.
- Sumac - 2 tablespoons.
- Olive oil - 2 tablespoons.
- Lemon juice - 1 lemon.
- Garlic cloves, minced - 2.
- Salt - to taste.
- Pepper - to taste.
- Onions, thinly sliced - 2.

Instructions

1. In a large bowl, mix the sumac, olive oil, lemon juice, garlic, salt, and pepper.

2. Add the chicken breasts and onions to the bowl, ensuring they are well coated with the marinade. Let it marinate for at least 1 hour.

3. Preheat the oven to 180°C (356°F).

4. Place the chicken and onions in a baking dish and bake for 25-30 minutes, or until the chicken is fully cooked.

5. Serve the chicken sliced, topped with the cooked onions.

CHICKEN AND LENTIL SOUP

Ingredients

- Chicken breasts, cubed - 500g.
- Red lentils, rinsed - 1 cup.
- Carrot, diced - 1.
- Onion, chopped - 1.
- Garlic cloves, minced - 2.
- Chicken stock - 6 cups.
- Cumin powder - 1 teaspoon.
- Turmeric powder - 1/2 teaspoon.
- Salt - to taste.
- Pepper - to taste.
- Lemon juice - 2 tablespoons.
- Fresh cilantro, chopped - for garnishing.

Instructions

1. In a large pot, add the chicken stock, cubed chicken, red lentils, carrot, onion, and garlic.

2. Bring to a boil, then reduce the heat to medium-low. Add cumin, turmeric, salt, and pepper.

3. Simmer for 25-30 minutes, or until the lentils are tender and the chicken is fully cooked.

4. Stir in lemon juice before serving.

5. Garnish with fresh cilantro. Serve hot.

CHICKEN AND CHICKPEA STEW

Ingredients

- Chicken thighs, boneless - 800g.
- Chickpeas, canned or soaked overnight - 1 cup.
- Onion, chopped - 1.
- Garlic cloves, minced - 3.
- Tomato paste - 2 tablespoons.
- Chicken stock - 4 cups.
- Paprika - 1 teaspoon.
- Cumin powder - 1 teaspoon.
- Salt - to taste.
- Pepper - to taste.
- Coriander, fresh - for garnishing.

Instructions

1. In a large pot, heat a bit of oil and brown the chicken thighs on both sides. Remove and set aside.

2. In the same pot, add onion and garlic, sautéing until translucent.

3. Stir in tomato paste, paprika, and cumin, cooking for a minute.

4. Add the chickpeas and chicken stock, bringing to a simmer.

5. Return the chicken to the pot. Season with salt and pepper.

6. Cover and simmer for 30-40 minutes, or until the chicken is tender.

7. Garnish with fresh coriander before serving.

CHICKEN FATTOUSH

Ingredients

- Chicken breasts, grilled and sliced - 400g.
- Romaine lettuce, chopped - 1 head.
- Cucumber, diced - 1.
- Tomatoes, diced - 2.
- Radishes, sliced - 5.
- Pita bread, toasted and broken into pieces - 2.
- Mint leaves, chopped - 1/4 cup.
- Sumac - 1 teaspoon.
- Lemon juice - 3 tablespoons.
- Olive oil - 1/4 cup.
- Salt - to taste.
- Pepper - to taste.

Instructions

1. In a large salad bowl, combine the lettuce, cucumber, tomatoes, radishes, and mint leaves.

2. Add the grilled and sliced chicken breasts to the salad.

3. In a small bowl, whisk together lemon juice, olive oil, sumac, salt, and pepper to make the dressing.

4. Pour the dressing over the salad and toss well to combine.

5. Just before serving, add the toasted pita pieces and gently toss again.

STUFFED CHICKEN WITH RICE

Ingredients

- Whole chicken - 1.5 kg.
- Basmati rice, soaked for 30 minutes - 2 cups.
- Ground beef - 200g.
- Almonds, toasted - 1/4 cup.
- Pine nuts, toasted - 1/4 cup.
- Onion, finely chopped - 1.
- Spices (cinnamon, cardamom, allspice) - 1 teaspoon each.
- Salt - to taste.
- Pepper - to taste.
- Butter - 2 tablespoons.
- Vegetable oil - for cooking.

Instructions

1. Preheat the oven to 190°C (375°F).

2. In a skillet, heat a bit of oil and cook the onions until translucent. Add the ground beef, half of the spices, salt, and pepper. Cook until the beef is browned.

3. Stir in the rice, almonds, pine nuts, and the rest of the spices, mixing well.

4. Stuff the chicken with the rice mixture and sew the opening closed or secure with skewers.

5. Rub the outside of the chicken with butter, and season with salt and pepper.

6. Roast in the preheated oven for about 1.5 hours, or until the chicken is fully cooked and the skin is golden brown.

7. Let the chicken rest for 10 minutes before carving. Serve with the remaining rice mixture on the side.

CHICKEN AND EGGPLANT STEW

Ingredients

- Chicken pieces - 1 kg.
- Eggplants, large, cut into cubes and salted - 2.
- Tomatoes, large, finely chopped - 3.
- Onion, finely chopped - 1.
- Garlic cloves, minced - 4.
- Chicken broth - 2 cups.
- Tomato paste - 2 tablespoons.
- Ground coriander - 1 teaspoon.
- Ground cumin - 1 teaspoon.
- Ground cinnamon - 1/2 teaspoon.
- Bay leaves - 2.
- Salt and pepper to taste.
- Olive oil - for frying.

Instructions

1. Heat the olive oil in a large pot over medium heat. Add the onions and garlic, sauté until they are soft.

2. Increase the heat to medium-high and add the chicken pieces to the pot. Brown them on all sides.

3. Stir in the tomato paste, chopped tomatoes, ground coriander, ground cumin, and ground cinnamon. Cook for 5 minutes, stirring frequently.

4. Add the chicken broth and bay leaves to the pot. Bring the mixture to a boil, then reduce the heat to low, cover, and simmer for 30 minutes.

5. While the stew is simmering, fry the eggplant cubes in a separate pan until they are golden brown. Once fried, add them to the stew.

6. Continue to simmer the stew, uncovered, for an additional 10 minutes, or until the chicken is fully cooked and the eggplants are tender. Season with salt and pepper to taste.

7. Remove the bay leaves before serving. Serve the stew hot with rice or flatbread.

SEAFOOD

Seafood in Iraqi cuisine emerges as a distinctive and cherished component, reflecting the country's geographical diversity and its access to both riverine and maritime resources. The use of fish and other seafood highlights a unique aspect of Iraqi culinary tradition, offering flavors and textures not found in other protein sources. Dishes such as masgouf, Iraq's national dish of grilled carp, exemplify the importance of seafood, showcasing the ability to blend simple ingredients with complex flavors derived from the Tigris and Euphrates rivers.

The nutritional profile of seafood is highly valued in Iraqi cuisine for its contribution to a healthy diet. Rich in omega-3 fatty acids, proteins, and essential nutrients like vitamins D and B2 (riboflavin), seafood offers a myriad of health benefits, including supporting heart health, brain function, and overall well-being. This emphasis on health is balanced with culinary techniques that enhance the natural flavors of the seafood, ensuring dishes are both nourishing and delicious.

Seafood's role in Iraqi cuisine extends beyond mere sustenance; it is a symbol of cultural heritage and dietary wisdom. Its preparation and consumption during meals underline the importance of diversity and nutritional balance, embodying the Iraqi approach to food that marries taste with health in every bite.

MASGOUF (GRILLED FISH)

Ingredients

- Carp or any large freshwater fish, cleaned and butterfly cut - 1.

- Olive oil - 4 tablespoons.
- Lime juice - 2 tablespoons.
- Salt and pepper to taste.
- Ground cumin - 1 teaspoon.
- Chopped fresh coriander - 2 tablespoons.
- Garlic cloves, minced - 2.
- Tomatoes, sliced - 2.
- Onions, sliced - 1.

Instructions

1. Preheat your grill to a medium-high heat.

2. Make deep slashes on both sides of the fish. Mix olive oil, lime juice, salt, pepper, ground cumin, and minced garlic in a bowl. Rub this mixture all over the fish, making sure it gets into the slashes.

3. Place the fish on the grill, skin side down. Grill for about 20-30 minutes, or until the fish is thoroughly cooked and the skin is crispy.

4. Halfway through grilling, add the sliced tomatoes and onions around the fish to cook.

5. Once done, remove from the grill and sprinkle with chopped fresh coriander. Serve with flatbread and lime wedges.

FISH BIRYANI

Ingredients

- Fish fillets, cut into pieces - 500g.
- Basmati rice, washed and soaked - 2 cups.
- Onions, thinly sliced - 2.
- Tomatoes, chopped - 2.

- Ginger-garlic paste - 1 tablespoon.
- Yogurt - 1/2 cup.
- Green chilies, slit - 2.
- Mint leaves, chopped - 1/4 cup.
- Cilantro, chopped - 1/4 cup.
- Biryani masala - 2 tablespoons.
- Turmeric powder - 1/2 teaspoon.
- Salt to taste.
- Lemon juice - 1 tablespoon.
- Saffron, soaked in warm milk - a pinch.
- Ghee - 2 tablespoons.

Instructions

1. Marinate the fish pieces with ginger-garlic paste, turmeric powder, lemon juice, and salt. Set aside for 30 minutes.

2. Heat ghee in a pan, add onions, and fry until golden brown. Remove half for garnishing later.

3. To the same pan, add tomatoes, green chilies, biryani masala, yogurt, mint, and cilantro. Cook until the oil separates.

4. Add the marinated fish to the pan and cook for about 10 minutes, or until the fish is cooked.

5. Cook the rice until it's 70% done. Layer the rice over the fish mixture. Sprinkle the saffron milk, fried onions, and some mint leaves on top.

6. Cover and cook on a low flame for 20 minutes. Mix gently before serving.

FISH KEBAB

Ingredients

- Fish fillets, minced - 500g.
- Onions, finely chopped - 1.
- Green chilies, finely chopped - 2.
- Ginger-garlic paste - 1 teaspoon.
- Garam masala - 1 teaspoon.
- Chopped cilantro - 2 tablespoons.
- Lemon juice - 1 tablespoon.
- Egg - 1.
- Bread crumbs - for coating.
- Salt to taste.
- Oil - for frying.

Instructions

1. In a bowl, combine the minced fish, onions, green chilies, ginger-garlic paste, garam masala, cilantro, lemon juice, and salt. Mix well.

2. Beat the egg and add to the fish mixture. This will help bind the kebabs.

3. Shape the mixture into kebabs, then roll them in bread crumbs.

4. Heat oil in a pan and fry the kebabs until golden brown on both sides.

5. Serve hot with mint chutney or ketchup.

FISH DOLMA

Ingredients

- Grape leaves, blanched - 30.
- Fish fillets, finely chopped - 500g.
- Rice, cooked - 1 cup.
- Onions, finely chopped - 2.
- Pine nuts - 1/4 cup.
- Dill, chopped - 2 tablespoons.
- Parsley, chopped - 2 tablespoons.
- Lemon juice - 2 tablespoons.
- Salt and pepper to taste.
- Olive oil - 2 tablespoons.

Instructions

1. In a large bowl, mix the chopped fish, cooked rice, onions, pine nuts, dill, parsley, lemon juice, salt, and pepper.

2. Lay out a grape leaf with the shiny side down. Place a small amount of the fish mixture in the center.

3. Fold in the sides and roll the leaf tightly into a small log. Repeat with the remaining leaves and filling.

4. Place the dolmas in a pot, seam side down. Drizzle with olive oil and enough water to cover.

5. Cover the pot and simmer for about 45 minutes. Serve warm or at room temperature.

FISH AND RICE SOUP

Ingredients

- Fish fillets, cut into pieces - 500g.
- Long-grain rice, washed - 1/2 cup.
- Onions, finely chopped - 1.
- Carrots, diced - 2.
- Celery stalks, diced - 2.
- Garlic cloves, minced - 2.
- Chicken or fish broth - 6 cups.
- Lemon juice - 2 tablespoons.
- Fresh dill, chopped - 2 tablespoons.
- Salt and pepper to taste.
- Olive oil - 2 tablespoons.

Instructions

1. Heat the olive oil in a large pot over medium heat. Add the onions, carrots, celery, and garlic. Sauté until the vegetables are soft.

2. Add the broth and bring to a boil. Stir in the rice, reduce the heat, and simmer for 15 minutes.

3. Add the fish pieces and continue to simmer for an additional 10 minutes, or until the fish is cooked through and the rice is tender.

4. Stir in the lemon juice and fresh dill. Season with salt and pepper to taste.

5. Serve the soup hot, garnished with more dill if desired.

SHRIMP BIRYANI

Ingredients

- Shrimp, peeled and deveined - 500g.
- Basmati rice, washed and soaked - 2 cups.
- Onions, thinly sliced - 2.
- Tomatoes, chopped - 2.
- Ginger-garlic paste - 1 tablespoon.
- Yogurt - 1/2 cup.
- Green chilies, slit - 2.
- Mint leaves, chopped - 1/4 cup.
- Cilantro, chopped - 1/4 cup.
- Biryani masala - 2 tablespoons.
- Turmeric powder - 1/2 teaspoon.
- Lemon juice - 1 tablespoon.
- Saffron, soaked in warm milk - a pinch.
- Ghee - 2 tablespoons.
- Salt to taste.

Instructions

1. Marinate the shrimp with ginger-garlic paste, turmeric powder, lemon juice, and salt. Set aside for 20 minutes.

2. In a large pan, heat ghee and fry onions until golden. Remove half for garnishing.

3. Add ginger-garlic paste to the pan and sauté for a minute. Add tomatoes, biryani masala, green chilies, mint, cilantro, and yogurt. Cook until oil separates.

4. Add marinated shrimp and cook for 5 minutes.

5. Layer the shrimp mixture with soaked rice. Top with saffron milk, fried onions, and a bit more ghee.

6. Cover and cook on low heat for 20 minutes or until the rice is done. Serve hot.

FISH SHAWARMA

Ingredients

- Fish fillets - 500g.
- Yogurt - 1 cup.
- Garlic cloves, minced - 4.
- Paprika - 1 teaspoon.
- Cumin powder - 1 teaspoon.
- Coriander powder - 1 teaspoon.
- Turmeric powder - 1/2 teaspoon.
- Lemon juice - 2 tablespoons.
- Salt and pepper to taste.
- Olive oil - 2 tablespoons.
- Tahini sauce - for serving.
- Pita bread - for serving.

Instructions

1. Mix yogurt, garlic, paprika, cumin, coriander, turmeric, lemon juice, salt, and pepper in a bowl.

2. Marinate the fish fillets in the mixture for at least 2 hours or overnight in the fridge.

3. Heat olive oil in a pan over medium heat. Add the marinated fish and cook until fully done, about 4-5 minutes per side.

4. Slice the cooked fish and serve in pita bread with tahini sauce and your choice of vegetables.

SHRIMP WITH RICE

Ingredients

- Shrimp, peeled and deveined - 400g.
- Basmati rice, washed - 1 cup.
- Onion, finely chopped - 1.
- Garlic cloves, minced - 2.
- Green peas - 1/2 cup.
- Carrots, diced - 1/2 cup.
- Cumin seeds - 1 teaspoon.
- Turmeric powder - 1/2 teaspoon.
- Chicken or vegetable broth - 2 cups.
- Salt and pepper to taste.
- Olive oil - 2 tablespoons.

Instructions

1. Heat olive oil in a pan, add cumin seeds and let them sizzle.

2. Add onions and garlic, sauté until soft.

3. Stir in rice, turmeric, salt, and pepper, and cook for a minute.

4. Add broth, bring to a boil, then reduce to a simmer. Cover and cook for 10 minutes.

5. Add shrimp, peas, and carrots. Cover and cook until the rice is done and shrimp are pink, about 10 more minutes.

6. Fluff with a fork and serve hot.

FISH AND TOMATO STEW

Ingredients

- Fish fillets - 500g.
- Tomatoes, chopped - 4.
- Onion, chopped - 1.
- Garlic cloves, minced - 3.
- Cumin powder - 1 teaspoon.
- Paprika - 1 teaspoon.
- Chicken or fish broth - 3 cups.
- Chopped cilantro - 1/4 cup.
- Salt and pepper to taste.
- Olive oil - 2 tablespoons.

Instructions

1. Heat olive oil in a large pot. Add onions and garlic, sauté until soft.

2. Add tomatoes, cumin, and paprika. Cook until tomatoes are soft.

3. Pour in broth and bring to a boil. Reduce heat and simmer for 10 minutes.

4. Add fish fillets and simmer until the fish is cooked through, about 10-15 minutes.

5. Season with salt and pepper. Garnish with cilantro before serving.

FRIED FISH WITH IRAQI SPICES

Ingredients

- Fish fillets - 500g.
- Flour - for coating.
- Curry powder - 2 teaspoons.
- Cumin powder - 1 teaspoon.
- Paprika - 1 teaspoon.
- Salt and pepper to taste.
- Lemon juice - 2 tablespoons.
- Vegetable oil - for frying.

Instructions

1. Season the fish fillets with salt, pepper, lemon juice, curry powder, cumin, and paprika.

2. Coat the seasoned fish fillets in flour.

3. Heat oil in a frying pan over medium heat. Fry the fish until golden brown on both sides and cooked through, about 4-5 minutes per side.

4. Serve hot with a side of rice or salad.

SEAFOOD WITH RICE

Ingredients

- Seafood mix (shrimp, squid, mussels) - 1 kg.
- Basmati rice, washed and soaked - 2 cups.
- Onions, finely chopped - 2.
- Garlic cloves, minced - 4.
- Tomatoes, chopped - 3.
- Green bell peppers, chopped - 1.
- Curry powder - 1 tablespoon.

- Cumin powder - 1 teaspoon.
- Turmeric powder - 1/2 teaspoon.
- Chicken or vegetable broth - 4 cups.
- Lemon juice - 2 tablespoons.
- Cilantro, chopped for garnish.
- Salt and pepper to taste.
- Vegetable oil - 2 tablespoons.

Instructions

1. Heat the oil in a large pot over medium heat. Add onions and garlic, sauté until golden.

2. Add tomatoes, bell peppers, curry powder, cumin, and turmeric. Cook until the tomatoes are soft.

3. Stir in the rice, then add the broth. Bring to a boil, reduce heat, cover, and simmer for 10 minutes.

4. Add the seafood mix, lemon juice, salt, and pepper. Cover and cook for an additional 10-15 minutes, or until the seafood is cooked through and the rice is tender.

5. Garnish with chopped cilantro before serving.

CLAM AND RICE SOUP

Ingredients

- Clams, cleaned - 500g.
- Basmati rice, washed - 1 cup.
- Onion, finely chopped - 1.
- Garlic cloves, minced - 2.
- Carrots, diced - 2.
- Chicken or fish broth - 6 cups.
- Fresh parsley, chopped - 2 tablespoons.
- Lemon juice - 1 tablespoon.

- Salt and pepper to taste.
- Olive oil - 1 tablespoon.

Instructions

1. Heat the olive oil in a large pot over medium heat. Add onion, garlic, and carrots. Sauté until the vegetables are soft.

2. Add the broth and bring to a boil. Add the rice, reduce heat, and simmer until the rice is halfway cooked, about 10 minutes.

3. Add the clams and cover the pot. Cook until the clams open, about 5-7 minutes.

4. Season with salt, pepper, and lemon juice. Stir in fresh parsley before serving.

FISH TIKKA

Ingredients

- Fish fillets (firm white fish like cod or haddock) - 500g.
- Yogurt - 1 cup.
- Ginger-garlic paste - 1 tablespoon.
- Chili powder - 1 teaspoon.
- Turmeric powder - 1/2 teaspoon.
- Garam masala - 1 teaspoon.
- Lemon juice - 2 tablespoons.
- Salt to taste.
- Vegetable oil - for brushing.

Instructions

1. In a bowl, mix yogurt, ginger-garlic paste, chili powder, turmeric, garam masala, lemon juice, and salt. Marinate the fish fillets in this mixture for at least 2 hours or overnight in the fridge.

2. Preheat your grill or oven to medium-high heat. Brush the grill grate or oven rack with oil.

3. Place the marinated fish on the grill or in the oven. Cook for about 3-4 minutes on each side or until the fish is cooked through and slightly charred.

4. Serve hot, garnished with lemon wedges and fresh cilantro.

SEAFOOD MASGOUF

Ingredients

- Large fish (carp, catfish, or similar), cleaned and butterflied - 1 whole.
- Olive oil - 3 tablespoons.
- Lemon juice - 2 tablespoons.
- Garlic cloves, minced - 4.
- Ground cumin - 1 teaspoon.
- Chili powder - 1 teaspoon.
- Salt and pepper to taste.
- Fresh coriander, chopped for garnish.

Instructions

1. Preheat your grill to a high heat.

2. Make several slashes on both sides of the fish. Mix olive oil, lemon juice, garlic, cumin, chili powder, salt, and

pepper in a bowl. Rub this mixture all over the fish, ensuring it gets into the slashes.

3. Place the fish on the grill, skin side down. Grill for 20-30 minutes, depending on the size of the fish, or until the flesh is tender and flakes easily.

4. Garnish with fresh coriander and serve with lemon wedges and Iraqi flatbread.

FISH AND LENTIL STEW

Ingredients

- Fish fillets, cut into chunks - 500g.
- Red lentils, rinsed - 1 cup.
- Onion, finely chopped - 1.
- Garlic cloves, minced - 2.
- Carrots, diced - 2.
- Celery stalks, chopped - 2.
- Tomatoes, diced - 2.
- Tomato paste - 2 tablespoons.
- Ground cumin - 1 teaspoon.
- Ground coriander - 1 teaspoon.
- Paprika - 1/2 teaspoon.
- Vegetable stock - 4 cups.
- Lemon juice - 1 tablespoon.
- Salt and pepper to taste.
- Olive oil - 2 tablespoons.
- Fresh cilantro, chopped for garnish.

Instructions

1. Heat olive oil in a large pot over medium heat. Add the onion, garlic, carrots, and celery. Cook until the vegetables are softened, about 5 minutes.

2. Stir in the ground cumin, ground coriander, and paprika. Cook for another minute until fragrant.

3. Add the red lentils, diced tomatoes, tomato paste, and vegetable stock. Bring to a boil, then reduce the heat to low, cover, and simmer for about 15 minutes.

4. Add the fish chunks to the pot. Season with salt and pepper. Cover and simmer for an additional 10-15 minutes, or until the fish is cooked through and the lentils are tender.

5. Stir in the lemon juice and adjust the seasoning if necessary.

6. Garnish with fresh cilantro before serving.

BREADS

Breads play a fundamental role in Iraqi cuisine, serving as both a staple food and a cultural emblem. They come in various forms, from the thin, soft lavash to the rich, doughy samoon, each type offering a different texture and taste to complement the array of Iraqi dishes. This variety not only showcases the culinary diversity within Iraq but also the skill and tradition passed down through generations, making bread an indispensable part of every meal.

Nutritionally, breads in Iraqi cuisine are a source of essential carbohydrates, providing the energy needed for daily activities. They often incorporate whole grains, lending fiber, vitamins, and minerals to the diet. The preparation of bread, often baked fresh daily, reflects a commitment to wholesome, nourishing food that supports a balanced diet while satisfying the palate.

In the context of Iraqi dining, bread transcends its role as a mere side dish; it is a vehicle for flavor and an integral part of the meal. Its presence on the table signifies hospitality and abundance, embodying the warmth and generosity that are hallmarks of Iraqi culture.

SAMOON

Ingredients

- All-purpose flour - 500g.
- Warm water - 300ml.
- Instant yeast - 2 teaspoons.
- Sugar - 1 tablespoon.
- Salt - 1 teaspoon.
- Olive oil - 2 tablespoons.

Instructions

1. In a large bowl, mix the flour, yeast, sugar, and salt.

2. Add the warm water and olive oil, and knead until the dough is smooth and elastic.

3. Cover the dough with a damp cloth and let it rise in a warm place for 1 hour, or until doubled in size.

4. Punch down the dough and divide it into 8 equal pieces. Shape each piece into an oval shape.

5. Place the shaped dough on a baking sheet lined with parchment paper, cover, and let them rise for another 30 minutes.

6. Preheat the oven to 220°C (428°F). Bake the samoon for 15-20 minutes or until golden brown.

KHUBZ (IRAQI FLATBREAD)

Ingredients

- All-purpose flour - 500g.
- Warm water - 300ml.
- Instant yeast - 1 teaspoon.
- Sugar - 1 teaspoon.
- Salt - 1 teaspoon.
- Olive oil - 2 tablespoons.

Instructions

1. Combine the flour, yeast, sugar, and salt in a large mixing bowl.

2. Gradually add the warm water and olive oil, mixing until a dough forms.

3. Knead the dough on a floured surface until smooth, about 10 minutes.

4. Place the dough in a greased bowl, cover with a cloth, and let it rise until doubled, about 1 hour.

5. Punch down the dough and divide it into small balls. Roll each ball into a thin circle.

6. Heat a skillet or griddle over medium heat. Cook each flatbread until it puffs up, then flip and cook the other side. Serve warm.

TANNOUR BREAD

Ingredients

- Whole wheat flour - 500g.
- Warm water - 350ml.
- Instant yeast - 2 teaspoons.
- Salt - 1 teaspoon.

Instructions

1. In a bowl, mix the whole wheat flour, yeast, and salt.

2. Add the warm water gradually and knead until a smooth, elastic dough forms.

3. Cover the dough and let it rise in a warm place for about 1-2 hours, until it doubles in size.

4. Divide the dough into small balls and roll each ball into a thin round.

5. Preheat your tannour or a cast-iron skillet over high heat. Place the rolled dough in the skillet and cook until bubbles form, then flip and cook the other side.

6. Serve the bread warm.

LAVASH

Ingredients

- All-purpose flour - 400g.
- Warm water - 250ml.
- Instant yeast - 1 teaspoon.
- Salt - 1/2 teaspoon.
- Sesame seeds or poppy seeds (optional) - for sprinkling.

Instructions

1. Mix the flour, yeast, and salt in a large bowl.

2. Add the warm water and mix until a dough forms.

3. Knead the dough for about 5 minutes until it's smooth.

4. Let the dough rest covered for about 30 minutes.

5. Preheat the oven to 230°C (446°F) and place a baking stone or inverted baking tray inside.

6. Divide the dough into small pieces and roll each piece out very thinly.

7. Transfer the rolled-out dough onto the hot baking stone or tray. Sprinkle with sesame or poppy seeds if using.

8. Bake until the lavash is lightly browned and crisp, about 3-5 minutes.

NAAN AL TAWA

Ingredients

- All-purpose flour - 500g.
- Warm milk - 250ml.
- Sugar - 1 tablespoon.
- Instant yeast - 1 teaspoon.
- Baking powder - 1/2 teaspoon.
- Salt - 1 teaspoon.
- Yogurt - 2 tablespoons.
- Oil - 2 tablespoons.

Instructions

1. In a large bowl, mix the flour, sugar, yeast, baking powder, and salt.

2. Add the warm milk, yogurt, and oil. Mix and knead into a soft dough.

3. Cover the dough and let it rise for 1 hour, until doubled in size.

4. Heat a tawa (flat skillet) on medium heat.

5. Divide the dough into balls, roll each ball into a circle or teardrop shape, and cook on the tawa until it puffs up. Flip and cook the other side.

6. Serve the naan warm, brushed with butter or ghee if desired.

IRAQI BAGUETTE

Ingredients

- All-purpose flour - 500g.
- Warm water - 320ml.
- Salt - 10g.
- Sugar - 15g.
- Instant yeast - 7g.
- Olive oil - 30ml.

Instructions

1. Combine the flour, salt, sugar, and instant yeast in a large mixing bowl.

2. Gradually add the warm water and olive oil, mixing until a dough forms.

3. Knead the dough on a lightly floured surface for about 10 minutes until it becomes smooth and elastic.

4. Place the dough in a lightly oiled bowl, cover with a damp cloth, and let it rise in a warm place for 1 hour or until it doubles in size.

5. Punch down the dough and divide it into two equal parts. Shape each part into a baguette and place on a baking sheet lined with parchment paper.

6. Preheat the oven to 230°C (450°F). Make several diagonal slashes on the top of each baguette with a sharp knife.

7. Bake in the preheated oven for 20-25 minutes or until the baguettes are golden brown and sound hollow when tapped on the bottom.

SAJ BREAD

Ingredients

- All-purpose flour - 400g.
- Warm water - 250ml.
- Instant yeast - 5g.
- Salt - 5g.
- Sugar - 10g.

Instructions

1. In a large bowl, mix together the flour, yeast, salt, and sugar.

2. Gradually add the warm water and mix until a dough starts to form.

3. Knead the dough on a floured surface for about 5-7 minutes until smooth and elastic.

4. Cover the dough and let it rise for about 1 hour, or until it has doubled in size.

5. Divide the dough into small balls and roll each ball out into a thin circle.

6. Heat a saj or large skillet over medium heat. Cook each bread for about 1-2 minutes on each side or until it puffs up and gets golden brown spots.

7. Serve the saj bread warm.

PITA BREAD

Ingredients

- All-purpose flour - 500g.
- Warm water - 300ml.
- Salt - 10g.
- Sugar - 5g.
- Instant yeast - 7g.
- Olive oil - 2 tablespoons.

Instructions

1. In a mixing bowl, combine the flour, yeast, salt, and sugar.

2. Add the warm water and olive oil, and mix until a dough forms.

3. Knead the dough for about 10 minutes until it's smooth and elastic.

4. Place the dough in a greased bowl, cover with a towel, and let it rise for 1 hour or until doubled in size.

5. Punch down the dough and divide it into 10-12 equal pieces. Roll each piece into a ball and then flatten into a disk.

6. Preheat the oven to 240°C (475°F) with a baking stone or inverted baking tray inside.

7. Roll each disk into a circle about 6 inches in diameter. Place on the hot stone or tray and bake for 2-3 minutes or until the bread puffs up.

8. Remove from the oven and wrap in a clean towel to keep soft. Serve warm.

KUBZ ZUBAIDI

Ingredients

- All-purpose flour - 500g.
- Warm water - 300ml.
- Instant yeast - 1 teaspoon.
- Salt - 1 teaspoon.
- Sugar - 1 tablespoon.

Instructions

1. Mix the flour, yeast, salt, and sugar in a large bowl.

2. Gradually add the warm water, mixing until a dough forms.

3. Knead the dough on a lightly floured surface until smooth and elastic, about 10 minutes.

4. Cover the dough and let it rise in a warm place for about 1 hour or until doubled in size.

5. Punch down the dough and divide it into small portions. Roll each portion into a ball, then flatten to form a round bread.

6. Preheat a baking stone or a heavy-duty baking sheet in the oven at 220°C (428°F).

7. Place the breads on the preheated stone or sheet and bake for about 10-12 minutes or until they are puffed and golden brown.

KUBZ MASGOUF

Ingredients

- All-purpose flour - 500g.
- Warm water - 320ml.
- Instant yeast - 2 teaspoons.
- Salt - 1 teaspoon.
- Sugar - 2 teaspoons.

Instructions

1. In a large bowl, combine the flour, yeast, salt, and sugar.

2. Add the warm water gradually, mixing to form a smooth dough.

3. Knead the dough on a floured surface until elastic, about 10 minutes.

4. Cover the dough with a damp cloth and let it rise in a warm place until doubled in size, about 1 hour.

5. Punch down the dough and divide it into equal-sized balls. Flatten each ball to form a disk.

6. Preheat an oven to 220°C (428°F) and place the disks on a baking sheet.

7. Bake for 10-15 minutes or until the breads are golden brown and puffed up.

CHEESE BREAD

Ingredients

- All-purpose flour - 500g.
- Warm milk - 250ml.
- Instant yeast - 1 tablespoon.
- Sugar - 1 teaspoon.
- Salt - 1 teaspoon.
- Melted butter - 50g.
- Shredded cheese (mozzarella or a mix) - 200g.
- Egg (for brushing) - 1.

Instructions

1. In a large bowl, combine the flour, yeast, sugar, and salt.

2. Add the warm milk and melted butter to the dry ingredients and knead until a smooth dough forms.

3. Cover the dough and let it rise in a warm place until doubled in size, about 1 hour.

4. Punch down the dough, then divide it into equal-sized balls. Flatten each ball, add a portion of shredded cheese in the center, and seal it by pinching the edges together.

5. Place the filled balls on a baking sheet lined with parchment paper, leaving some space between each. Let them rise again for about 30 minutes.

6. Preheat the oven to 180°C (356°F). Brush the tops of the bread with beaten egg.

7. Bake for 20-25 minutes, or until golden brown. Serve warm.

SESAME BREAD

Ingredients

- All-purpose flour - 500g.
- Warm water - 300ml.
- Instant yeast - 2 teaspoons.
- Sugar - 2 tablespoons.
- Salt - 1 teaspoon.
- Olive oil - 2 tablespoons.
- Sesame seeds - 100g.

Instructions

1. In a mixing bowl, combine flour, yeast, sugar, and salt.

2. Gradually add the warm water and olive oil to the dry ingredients, mixing until a dough forms.

3. Knead the dough on a floured surface until smooth and elastic, about 10 minutes.

4. Place the dough in a greased bowl, cover, and let it rise until doubled, about 1 hour.

5. Punch down the dough and shape it into a loaf or individual rolls. Wet the surface with a little water and sprinkle generously with sesame seeds.

6. Preheat the oven to 200°C (392°F). Place the bread on a baking sheet and let it rise again for about 30 minutes.

7. Bake for 25-30 minutes or until golden brown. Cool on a wire rack before serving.

OLIVE BREAD

Ingredients

- All-purpose flour - 500g.
- Warm water - 300ml.
- Instant yeast - 2 teaspoons.
- Sugar - 1 tablespoon.
- Salt - 1 teaspoon.
- Chopped black olives - 150g.
- Dried oregano - 2 teaspoons.

Instructions

1. Mix the flour, yeast, sugar, and salt in a large bowl.

2. Add warm water to the dry ingredients and knead to form a soft dough.

3. Fold in the chopped olives and oregano until evenly distributed.

4. Let the dough rise in a warm place until doubled in size, about 1 hour.

5. Shape the dough into a loaf and place it on a baking sheet lined with parchment paper.

6. Allow to rise for an additional 30 minutes. Preheat the oven to 200°C (392°F).

7. Bake for 30-35 minutes or until the bread sounds hollow when tapped on the bottom. Let cool before slicing.

ZATAR BREAD

Ingredients

- All-purpose flour - 500g.
- Warm water - 300ml.
- Instant yeast - 2 teaspoons.
- Sugar - 1 tablespoon.
- Salt - 1 teaspoon.
- Za'atar mix - 100g.
- Olive oil - for brushing.

Instructions

1. In a large bowl, mix together the flour, yeast, sugar, and salt.

2. Gradually add the warm water to the dry ingredients and knead until a smooth dough forms.

3. Cover the dough and let it rise in a warm place until doubled in size, about 1 hour.

4. Divide the dough into balls. Roll each ball into a circle and place on a baking sheet.

5. Brush the top of each dough circle with olive oil and sprinkle a generous amount of za'atar mix on top.

6. Preheat the oven to 220°C (428°F). Let the dough rest for 15 minutes before baking.

7. Bake for 10-15 minutes or until the edges are golden brown. Serve warm.

SWEET BREAD (KLEICHA)

Ingredients

- All-purpose flour - 500g.
- Warm milk - 200ml.
- Butter, melted - 100g.
- Instant yeast - 2 teaspoons.
- Sugar - 100g.
- Egg - 1 (for the dough).
- Cardamom powder - 1 teaspoon.
- Filling: Dates, pitted and mashed - 200g.
- Cinnamon powder - 1 teaspoon (for filling).
- Nutmeg - 1/2 teaspoon (for filling).
- Egg yolk - 1 (for brushing).
- Sesame seeds - for sprinkling.

Instructions

1. Combine flour, yeast, sugar, and cardamom in a large bowl.

2. Mix in the warm milk, melted butter, and egg until a dough forms.

3. Knead the dough on a floured surface until smooth. Let it rise in a warm place for 1 hour.

4. For the filling, mix the mashed dates with cinnamon and nutmeg.

5. Roll out the dough and spread the date mixture over it. Roll it up and cut into pieces.

6. Place the pieces on a baking sheet, brush with egg yolk, and sprinkle with sesame seeds.

7. Preheat the oven to 180°C (356°F). Bake for 20-25 minutes or until golden.

CONDIMENTS

Condiments in Iraqi cuisine play a crucial role in adding depth and complexity to dishes, elevating the flavors of the main ingredients. These range from tangy pickles and spicy salsas to rich tahini and aromatic herb blends, each contributing its unique profile to create a harmonious balance on the palate. Their use demonstrates the intricacy of Iraqi culinary art, where the interplay of flavors is key to achieving the signature taste that defines the cuisine.

Nutritionally, these condiments are not just flavor enhancers but also offer health benefits. Many are made from natural ingredients like herbs, spices, fruits, and vegetables, packed with vitamins, minerals, and antioxidants. The traditional methods of preparing these condiments, such as fermenting and blending, preserve their nutritional value, making them a beneficial addition to a healthy diet.

The inclusion of condiments in Iraqi meals underscores the cuisine's emphasis on diversity and complexity. They serve as a testament to the rich culinary heritage of Iraq, highlighting the importance of each component in creating dishes that are not only flavorful but also nutritiously balanced.

AMBA (MANGO PICKLE)

Ingredients

- Green mangoes, peeled and thinly sliced - 2.
- Fenugreek seeds - 1 teaspoon.
- Mustard seeds - 1 teaspoon.
- Turmeric powder - 1 teaspoon.
- Chili powder - 1 tablespoon.

- Salt - 2 tablespoons.
- Vinegar - 1 cup.
- Sugar - 1 tablespoon.
- Water - 2 cups.

Instructions

1. In a saucepan, combine the water, vinegar, and sugar. Bring to a boil, then add the mango slices. Cook for about 5 minutes until the mangoes are soft.

2. In a separate pan, dry roast the fenugreek and mustard seeds until they start to pop. Grind them into a powder.

3. Add the ground fenugreek and mustard seeds to the mangoes, along with turmeric, chili powder, and salt. Mix well.

4. Simmer the mixture for another 10-15 minutes until thickened.

5. Let it cool, then transfer to sterilized jars. Store in the refrigerator.

TAMARIND SAUCE

Ingredients

- Tamarind paste - 1/4 cup.
- Water - 1 cup.
- Sugar - 2 tablespoons.
- Salt - 1/2 teaspoon.
- Cumin powder - 1 teaspoon.
- Chili powder - 1/2 teaspoon (optional).

Instructions

1. In a small saucepan, mix the tamarind paste and water. Bring to a simmer over medium heat.

2. Add sugar, salt, cumin powder, and chili powder. Stir well.

3. Simmer the sauce for 5-10 minutes, or until it thickens slightly.

4. Let the sauce cool, then strain it to remove any solids. Store in a sealed container in the refrigerator.

GARLIC YOGURT SAUCE

Ingredients

- Plain yogurt - 1 cup.
- Garlic, minced - 2 cloves.
- Lemon juice - 1 tablespoon.
- Salt - to taste.
- Fresh mint, chopped - 1 tablespoon (optional).

Instructions

1. In a bowl, combine the yogurt, minced garlic, lemon juice, and salt. Mix well.

2. Add the chopped mint if using and stir to combine.

3. Refrigerate for at least 30 minutes before serving to allow the flavors to meld.

TAHINI SAUCE

Ingredients

- Tahini (sesame paste) - 1/2 cup.
- Water - 1/4 cup.
- Lemon juice - 3 tablespoons.
- Garlic, minced - 1 clove.
- Salt - to taste.
- Parsley, finely chopped - 2 tablespoons (optional).

Instructions

1. In a bowl, whisk together the tahini and lemon juice. The mixture will thicken and become lighter in color.

2. Gradually add water until the sauce reaches your desired consistency.

3. Stir in the minced garlic and salt. Adjust the seasoning as needed.

4. Garnish with chopped parsley if using. Serve with grilled meats, vegetables, or as a salad dressing.

POMEGRANATE MOLASSES

Ingredients

- Pomegranate juice - 4 cups.
- Sugar - 1/2 cup.
- Lemon juice - 2 tablespoons.

Instructions

1. In a large saucepan, combine the pomegranate juice, sugar, and lemon juice. Stir well.

2. Bring the mixture to a boil, then reduce the heat and simmer, stirring occasionally, until the mixture reduces to about 1 cup and has a syrup-like consistency, approximately 70-80 minutes.

3. Allow the molasses to cool, then transfer to a jar. It will thicken further upon cooling. Store in the refrigerator.

IRAQI CHILI PASTE

Ingredients

- Red chili peppers, chopped - 200g.
- Garlic cloves, minced - 4.
- Tomato paste - 2 tablespoons.
- Ground cumin - 1 teaspoon.
- Salt - 1 teaspoon.
- Olive oil - 2 tablespoons.
- Vinegar - 1 tablespoon.

Instructions

1. Combine the chopped chili peppers, minced garlic, tomato paste, ground cumin, and salt in a food processor.

2. Pulse until the ingredients form a smooth paste.

3. Transfer the paste to a bowl, and mix in the olive oil and vinegar until well combined.

4. Store the chili paste in a sterilized jar in the refrigerator.

PICKLED VEGETABLES

Ingredients

- Cauliflower florets - 1 cup.
- Carrots, sliced - 1 cup.
- Green beans - 1 cup.
- Garlic cloves - 4.
- Water - 2 cups.
- Vinegar - 1 cup.
- Salt - 2 tablespoons.
- Sugar - 1 teaspoon.
- Mustard seeds - 1 teaspoon.
- Coriander seeds - 1 teaspoon.

Instructions

1. In a large pot, bring water, vinegar, salt, sugar, mustard seeds, and coriander seeds to a boil.

2. Add the cauliflower, carrots, green beans, and garlic cloves to the boiling mixture.

3. Lower the heat and simmer for 5 minutes.

4. Transfer the vegetables and brine into sterilized jars.

5. Let the jars cool to room temperature, then seal and store in the refrigerator.

MINT CHUTNEY

Ingredients

- Fresh mint leaves - 1 cup.
- Garlic cloves - 2.
- Green chili - 1.

- Lemon juice - 2 tablespoons.
- Salt - 1/2 teaspoon.
- Water - 1/4 cup.

Instructions

1. Combine the mint leaves, garlic, green chili, lemon juice, salt, and water in a blender.

2. Blend until the mixture forms a smooth chutney.

3. Adjust the salt and lemon juice to taste.

4. Transfer the chutney to a jar and refrigerate until ready to use.

OLIVE TAPENADE

Ingredients

- Pitted black olives - 1 cup.
- Capers, rinsed - 2 tablespoons.
- Anchovy fillets (optional) - 2.
- Garlic clove - 1.
- Fresh lemon juice - 1 tablespoon.
- Olive oil - 3 tablespoons.
- Fresh parsley, chopped - 1 tablespoon.

Instructions

1. In a food processor, combine the black olives, capers, anchovy fillets, and garlic clove.

2. Pulse until the ingredients are finely chopped.

3. With the processor running, gradually add the lemon juice and olive oil until the mixture becomes a coarse paste.

4. Stir in the chopped parsley.

5. Transfer the tapenade to a jar and store in the refrigerator until needed.

DATE SYRUP

Ingredients

- Pitted dates - 1 cup.
- Water - 2 cups.
- Lemon juice - 1 tablespoon.

Instructions

1. Combine the dates and water in a saucepan. Bring to a simmer over medium heat.

2. Cook for 20-30 minutes, or until the dates are very soft and the water has reduced by half.

3. Remove from heat and let cool slightly.

4. Blend the mixture with lemon juice until smooth.

5. Strain the syrup through a fine mesh sieve to remove any solids.

6. Store the date syrup in a sterilized jar in the refrigerator.

WALNUT AND POMEGRANATE PASTE

Ingredients

- Walnuts, finely ground - 1 cup.
- Pomegranate molasses - 3 tablespoons.
- Garlic, minced - 1 clove.
- Salt - 1/2 teaspoon.
- Red pepper flakes - 1/4 teaspoon (optional).

Instructions

1. In a mixing bowl, combine the finely ground walnuts, pomegranate molasses, minced garlic, salt, and red pepper flakes if using. Mix until well combined.

2. Taste and adjust the seasoning if necessary. The paste should have a tangy, slightly sweet, and nutty flavor.

3. Transfer the paste to a serving dish and let it rest for at least an hour to allow the flavors to meld together.

4. Serve as a condiment with grilled meats, fish, or as a spread on bread.

EGGPLANT DIP

Ingredients

- Eggplants, large - 2.
- Tahini - 2 tablespoons.
- Lemon juice - 2 tablespoons.
- Garlic, minced - 2 cloves.
- Olive oil - 2 tablespoons.
- Salt - to taste.
- Parsley, chopped for garnish.

Instructions

1. Preheat your oven to 200°C (400°F). Prick the eggplants with a fork and place them on a baking sheet. Roast until the skin is charred and the inside is soft, about 30-40 minutes.

2. Once cool enough to handle, peel the eggplants and place the flesh in a colander to drain any excess liquid.

3. In a bowl, mash the eggplant with a fork or blend in a food processor for a smoother texture.

4. Add the tahini, lemon juice, minced garlic, olive oil, and salt. Mix until well combined.

5. Adjust the seasoning as needed, garnish with chopped parsley, and drizzle with a bit more olive oil before serving.

CUCUMBER PICKLE

Ingredients

- Cucumbers, thinly sliced - 3.
- Water - 1 cup.
- Vinegar - 1/2 cup.
- Sugar - 2 tablespoons.
- Salt - 1 tablespoon.
- Dill, fresh or dried - 1 teaspoon.
- Garlic cloves, sliced - 2.

Instructions

1. In a saucepan, bring water, vinegar, sugar, and salt to a boil, stirring until the sugar and salt are dissolved.

2. Place the sliced cucumbers, dill, and garlic in a clean jar.

3. Pour the hot vinegar mixture over the cucumbers, ensuring they are completely covered.

4. Allow the mixture to cool to room temperature, then seal the jar and refrigerate for at least 24 hours before serving.

LEMON AND OLIVE OIL DRESSING

Ingredients

- Olive oil - 1/2 cup.
- Lemon juice - 1/4 cup.
- Garlic, minced - 1 clove.
- Salt - 1/2 teaspoon.
- Black pepper, freshly ground - 1/4 teaspoon.

Instructions

1. In a small bowl, whisk together olive oil, lemon juice, minced garlic, salt, and black pepper until well combined.

2. Taste and adjust the seasoning if necessary. The dressing should have a balanced flavor of tartness from the lemon and richness from the olive oil.

3. Use immediately or store in a sealed container in the refrigerator. Shake well before each use.

SUMAC SPICE MIX

Ingredients

- Sumac - 1/4 cup.
- Sesame seeds, toasted - 2 tablespoons.
- Thyme, dried - 1 tablespoon.
- Marjoram, dried - 1 teaspoon.
- Oregano, dried - 1 teaspoon.
- Salt - 1/2 teaspoon.

Instructions

1. In a small bowl, mix together the sumac, toasted sesame seeds, thyme, marjoram, oregano, and salt until well combined.

2. Store the spice mix in an airtight container at room temperature.

3. Use as a seasoning for meats, vegetables, or as a topping for dips and salads to add a tangy, lemony flavor.

DESSERTS

Desserts in Iraqi cuisine offer a delightful conclusion to meals, showcasing an array of sweet treats that range from rich pastries to light, fruit-based dishes. These confections are deeply rooted in the country's traditions, featuring ingredients like dates, nuts, and honey, which not only provide sweetness but also cultural significance. The variety of desserts reflects the creativity and richness of Iraqi culinary heritage, where each sweet dish tells a story of gatherings, celebrations, and everyday pleasures.

Nutritionally, while desserts are often indulgent, many Iraqi sweets incorporate healthful elements. Dates, for instance, are a common ingredient, offering natural sweetness along with fiber, vitamins, and minerals. Nuts and seeds add texture and are a source of healthy fats and protein, making these desserts not only enjoyable but also a source of nourishment.

The role of desserts in Iraqi cuisine goes beyond mere indulgence; they are an expression of hospitality and joy. Serving these sweets to guests is a sign of welcome and generosity, reflecting the importance of food in bringing people together and celebrating life's moments.

BAKLAVA

Ingredients

- Phyllo dough - 1 package.
- Unsalted butter, melted - 1 cup.
- Walnuts, finely chopped - 2 cups.
- Sugar - 1 cup.
- Cinnamon powder - 1 teaspoon.
- For the syrup:
- Water - 1 cup.

- Sugar - 1 cup.
- Honey - 1/2 cup.
- Lemon juice - 2 tablespoons.
- Vanilla extract - 1 teaspoon.

Instructions

1. Preheat the oven to 175°C (350°F).

2. Brush a 9x13 inch baking pan with melted butter. Lay a sheet of phyllo dough in the pan and brush with butter. Repeat with 8 more sheets.

3. Mix the walnuts, sugar, and cinnamon. Sprinkle a third of this mixture over the phyllo in the pan.

4. Add 5 more buttered sheets of phyllo, then another third of the walnut mixture. Repeat once more, finishing with a top layer of 8 buttered phyllo sheets.

5. Cut into diamond or square shapes with a sharp knife.

6. Bake for about 50 minutes, or until golden and crisp.

7. While the baklava is baking, make the syrup by boiling water and sugar until sugar is dissolved. Add honey and lemon juice, simmer for about 20 minutes. Stir in vanilla extract.

8. Remove baklava from oven and immediately pour the syrup over it. Let cool completely before serving.

KLEICHA (DATE COOKIES)

Ingredients

- All-purpose flour - 3 cups.
- Unsalted butter, melted - 1 cup.
- Sugar - 1/2 cup.
- Active dry yeast - 1 teaspoon.
- Warm water - 1/2 cup.
- For the filling:
- Dates, pitted and mashed - 2 cups.
- Cardamom powder - 1 teaspoon.
- Walnuts, chopped (optional) - 1/2 cup.

Instructions

1. Dissolve yeast in warm water with a teaspoon of sugar. Let it sit until frothy, about 10 minutes.

2. In a large bowl, mix flour and sugar. Add the yeast mixture and melted butter. Knead until smooth. Let the dough rise in a warm place for 1 hour.

3. Preheat the oven to 180°C (356°F).

4. Roll out the dough on a floured surface. Spread the date mixture over the dough, then roll it up.

5. Cut into 1-inch pieces and place on a baking sheet. Bake for 20-25 minutes or until golden.

HALAWA (HALVA)

Ingredients

- Tahini (sesame paste) - 2 cups.
- Sugar - 2 cups.

- Water - 1 cup.
- Lemon juice - 1 tablespoon.
- Vanilla extract - 1 teaspoon.
- Pistachios, chopped - 1/2 cup.

Instructions

1. In a saucepan, heat sugar and water over medium heat until the sugar dissolves. Add lemon juice and simmer until it reaches a thick syrup consistency.

2. Remove from heat and gradually add the tahini, stirring continuously until the mixture becomes smooth.

3. Stir in vanilla extract and pistachios.

4. Pour the mixture into a greased pan and let it cool. Refrigerate until set, then cut into squares or diamonds.

ZNOUD-EL-SIT

Ingredients

- Phyllo dough - 1 package.
- Unsalted butter, melted - 1 cup.
- For the filling:
- Ricotta cheese - 2 cups.
- Sugar - 1/4 cup.
- Orange blossom water - 1 tablespoon.
- For the syrup:
- Water - 1 cup.
- Sugar - 1 cup.
- Lemon juice - 1 tablespoon.
- Rose water - 1 teaspoon.

Instructions

1. Preheat the oven to 180°C (356°F).

2. Mix the ricotta cheese, sugar, and orange blossom water for the filling.

3. Cut phyllo dough into strips, brush with melted butter, place a spoonful of filling at one end and roll up, tucking in the sides.

4. Place the rolls on a baking sheet, brush with more butter, and bake until golden, about 20 minutes.

5. Prepare the syrup by boiling water and sugar, adding lemon juice, and simmering until thickened. Stir in rose water.

6. Pour the syrup over the baked znoud-el-sit while still hot. Let soak before serving.

QATAYEF (STUFFED PANCAKES)

Ingredients

- All-purpose flour - 2 cups.
- Instant yeast - 1 tsp.
- Baking powder - 1 tsp.
- Sugar - 2 tbsp.
- Warm water - 1 1/2 cups.
- Salt - a pinch.
- For the filling: Walnuts, chopped - 1 cup.
- Cinnamon powder - 1 tsp.
- Sugar - 2 tbsp.
- For the syrup: Sugar - 2 cups.
- Water - 1 cup.
- Lemon juice - 1 tbsp.

- Rose water - 1 tsp.

Instructions

1. In a large bowl, mix the flour, yeast, baking powder, sugar, and salt. Gradually add the warm water and mix until the batter is smooth. Let it rest for 30 minutes.

2. Heat a non-stick pan over medium heat. Pour a small amount of batter to form a pancake. Cook until the surface is bubbly and the edges are dry, but do not flip. Remove and place on a plate. Repeat with the remaining batter.

3. Mix the walnuts, cinnamon, and sugar for the filling.

4. When the pancakes have cooled slightly, add a spoonful of the walnut mixture to the center of each pancake. Fold in half and press the edges together to seal.

5. To make the syrup, combine sugar, water, and lemon juice in a saucepan. Bring to a boil, then reduce heat and simmer for 10 minutes. Add the rose water and let it cool.

6. Fry the stuffed pancakes in hot oil until golden brown. Drain on paper towels.

7. Dip the fried qatayef in the syrup or drizzle the syrup over them before serving.

BASBOUSA

Ingredients

- Semolina - 2 cups.
- Desiccated coconut - 1 cup.
- Sugar - 1 cup.

- Yogurt - 1 cup.
- Baking powder - 1 teaspoon.
- Butter, melted - 3/4 cup.
- Almonds or pistachios for garnish.
- For the syrup:
- Sugar - 1 1/2 cups.
- Water - 1 cup.
- Lemon juice - 1 tablespoon.
- Rose water - 1 teaspoon.

Instructions

1. Preheat the oven to 180°C (356°F).

2. In a large bowl, mix together the semolina, coconut, sugar, yogurt, baking powder, and melted butter until well combined.

3. Spread the mixture in a greased baking tray. Smooth the top with a wet spoon.

4. Score the top into diamond shapes and place an almond or pistachio in the center of each diamond.

5. Bake for 30-35 minutes, or until golden brown.

6. While the basbousa is baking, prepare the syrup by combining sugar, water, and lemon juice in a saucepan. Bring to a boil, then simmer for 10 minutes. Add rose water and remove from heat.

7. Pour the hot syrup over the hot basbousa as soon as it comes out of the oven.

8. Allow to cool before serving.

MAAMOUL (STUFFED COOKIES)

Ingredients

- For the dough:
- All-purpose flour - 3 cups.
- Fine semolina - 1 cup.
- Butter, melted - 1 cup.
- Powdered sugar - 1/2 cup.
- Rose water - 1/4 cup.
- For the filling:
- Dates, pitted and chopped - 2 cups.
- Walnuts, chopped - 1 cup.
- Cinnamon powder - 1 teaspoon.
- Powdered sugar for dusting.

Instructions

1. Mix flour and semolina in a large bowl. Add melted butter and mix well. Gradually add rose water until a dough forms. Cover and rest for an hour.

2. For the filling, mix dates, walnuts, and cinnamon.

3. Preheat oven to 180°C (356°F).

4. Take a piece of dough, flatten it, place some filling in the center, and seal it into a ball. Shape as desired using a maamoul mold.

5. Place on a baking sheet and bake for 15-20 minutes or until lightly golden.

6. Cool on a wire rack and dust with powdered sugar before serving.

RICE PUDDING

Ingredients

- Milk - 4 cups.
- Short grain rice, washed and soaked - 1/2 cup.
- Sugar - 3/4 cup.
- Rose water - 1 tablespoon.
- Ground cardamom - 1/2 teaspoon.
- Pistachios for garnish.

Instructions

1. In a large saucepan, bring the milk to a boil. Add the rice and reduce the heat to low.

2. Simmer for 20-25 minutes, stirring occasionally, until the rice is cooked and the mixture has thickened.

3. Add the sugar, rose water, and cardamom. Cook for another 5 minutes.

4. Pour into serving dishes and allow to cool. Refrigerate until set.

5. Garnish with pistachios before serving.

MUHALLABIA (MILK PUDDING)

Ingredients

- Milk - 4 cups.
- Cornstarch - 1/4 cup.
- Sugar - 1/2 cup.
- Rose water - 2 tablespoons.
- Pistachios, chopped for garnish.

Instructions

1. Mix the cornstarch with 1/2 cup of milk until smooth.

2. Heat the remaining milk and sugar in a saucepan. When it starts to boil, add the cornstarch mixture.

3. Stir continuously until the mixture thickens.

4. Remove from heat and add the rose water.

5. Pour into serving dishes and allow to cool. Refrigerate until set.

6. Garnish with chopped pistachios before serving.

IRAQI CARDAMOM COOKIES

Ingredients

- Butter, softened - 1 cup.
- Powdered sugar - 1 cup.
- Cardamom, ground - 2 teaspoons.
- All-purpose flour - 2 1/2 cups.
- Pistachios, chopped for garnish.

Instructions

1. Preheat the oven to 180°C (356°F).

2. Cream together the butter and powdered sugar until light and fluffy.

3. Mix in the ground cardamom.

4. Gradually add the flour, mixing until a dough forms.

5. Shape the dough into small balls and place on a baking sheet. Press a pistachio into the top of each ball.

6. Bake for 10-12 minutes or until lightly golden.

7. Cool on a wire rack before serving.

DATE AND WALNUT ROLL

Ingredients

- Dates, pitted - 2 cups.
- Walnuts, chopped - 1 cup.
- Butter - 2 tablespoons.
- Cardamom powder - 1/2 teaspoon.
- Desiccated coconut for coating.

Instructions

1. In a food processor, blend the dates, walnuts, butter, and cardamom powder until the mixture forms a sticky dough.

2. Transfer the dough onto a piece of parchment paper and shape into a log.

3. Roll the log in desiccated coconut until fully coated.

4. Chill in the refrigerator for 2 hours, then slice into rounds before serving.

SAFFRON ICE CREAM

Ingredients

- Heavy cream - 2 cups.
- Milk - 1 cup.

- Sugar - 3/4 cup.
- Saffron threads - 1/2 teaspoon.
- Pistachios, chopped - 1/4 cup.
- Rose water - 1 tablespoon.

Instructions

1. In a saucepan, combine milk, cream, and saffron. Heat over medium heat until it just begins to simmer, then remove from heat.

2. In a separate bowl, whisk the sugar into the milk mixture until dissolved.

3. Stir in the rose water and let the mixture cool completely.

4. Pour into an ice cream maker and churn according to the manufacturer's instructions.

5. Once churned, fold in the chopped pistachios, then transfer to a freezer-safe container and freeze until firm.

PISTACHIO BAKLAVA

Ingredients

- Phyllo dough - 1 package.
- Unsalted butter, melted - 1 cup.
- Pistachios, finely chopped - 2 cups.
- Sugar - 1 cup.
- Water - 1 cup.
- Honey - 1/2 cup.
- Lemon juice - 2 tablespoons.
- Cinnamon stick - 1.

Instructions

1. Preheat the oven to 180°C (356°F).

2. Brush a baking dish with melted butter. Layer half of the phyllo sheets, brushing each sheet with melted butter.

3. Mix the chopped pistachios with 1/4 cup of sugar and spread over the layered phyllo.

4. Layer the remaining phyllo sheets on top, brushing each with butter.

5. Cut into diamonds or squares and bake for 50 minutes, or until golden and crisp.

6. While baking, prepare the syrup by boiling water, the remaining sugar, honey, lemon juice, and cinnamon stick for 10 minutes.

7. Remove the cinnamon stick and pour the hot syrup over the hot baklava.

8. Let it cool completely before serving.

SEMOLINA CAKE

Ingredients

- Semolina - 2 cups.
- Sugar - 1 cup.
- Yogurt - 1 cup.
- Baking powder - 2 teaspoons.
- Butter, melted - 1/2 cup.
- Almonds for garnish.
- For the syrup:

- Sugar - 1 1/2 cups.
- Water - 1 cup.
- Lemon juice - 1 tablespoon.
- Rose water - 1 teaspoon.

Instructions

1. Preheat the oven to 180°C (356°F).

2. In a bowl, mix the semolina, sugar, yogurt, baking powder, and melted butter until well combined.

3. Pour the batter into a greased baking dish, and smooth the top. Press almonds into the batter.

4. Bake for 30-35 minutes or until golden brown.

5. Prepare the syrup by boiling sugar, water, and lemon juice for 10 minutes, then add rose water.

6. Pour the hot syrup over the hot cake. Let it absorb the syrup before serving.

ROSE WATER PUDDING

Ingredients

- Cornstarch - 1/4 cup.
- Water - 1/4 cup.
- Milk - 2 cups.
- Sugar - 1/2 cup.
- Rose water - 2 tablespoons.
- Pistachios, chopped for garnish.

Instructions

1. Dissolve the cornstarch in water in a small bowl.

2. In a saucepan, heat the milk and sugar over medium heat, stirring until the sugar is dissolved.

3. Add the cornstarch mixture to the milk, stirring constantly until the mixture thickens.

4. Remove from heat and stir in the rose water.

5. Pour into serving dishes and refrigerate until set, about 2 hours.

6. Garnish with chopped pistachios before serving.

FIG AND HONEY CAKE

Ingredients

- Dried figs, chopped - 1 cup.
- Boiling water - 1 cup.
- All-purpose flour - 2 cups.
- Baking powder - 1 teaspoon.
- Baking soda - 1/2 teaspoon.
- Salt - 1/4 teaspoon.
- Cinnamon powder - 1 teaspoon.
- Honey - 3/4 cup.
- Vegetable oil - 1/2 cup.
- Eggs - 2.
- Vanilla extract - 1 teaspoon.

Instructions

1. Preheat the oven to 175°C (350°F). Grease and flour a 9-inch round cake pan.

2. Pour boiling water over chopped figs in a bowl and let them soak for 10 minutes. Drain any excess water.

3. In a separate bowl, whisk together flour, baking powder, baking soda, salt, and cinnamon.

4. In a large bowl, mix honey, oil, eggs, and vanilla extract. Stir in the figs.

5. Gradually add the dry ingredients to the wet ingredients, stirring until just combined.

6. Pour the batter into the prepared pan and bake for 30-35 minutes, or until a toothpick inserted into the center comes out clean.

7. Let the cake cool before serving. Drizzle with additional honey if desired.

SWEET CHEESE PASTRY

Ingredients

- Filo pastry sheets - 10.
- Unsalted butter, melted - 1/2 cup.
- For the filling:
- Ricotta cheese - 2 cups.
- Sugar - 1/2 cup.
- Egg - 1.
- Vanilla extract - 1 teaspoon.
- For the syrup:
- Sugar - 1 cup.
- Water - 1/2 cup.
- Lemon juice - 1 tablespoon.
- Rose water - 1 teaspoon.

Instructions

1. Preheat the oven to 180°C (356°F). Grease a 9x13 inch baking dish.

2. To make the filling, mix ricotta cheese, sugar, egg, and vanilla extract in a bowl until well combined.

3. Lay one sheet of filo pastry in the prepared dish, brush with melted butter, and repeat with 4 more sheets.

4. Spread the cheese mixture over the layered filo. Cover with 5 more filo sheets, brushing each with butter.

5. Cut the pastry into squares or diamonds before baking. Bake for 30-35 minutes or until golden brown.

6. While the pastry is baking, prepare the syrup by boiling sugar, water, and lemon juice for 10 minutes. Add rose water and let cool.

7. Pour the cooled syrup over the hot pastry. Let it absorb the syrup for a few hours before serving.

ALMOND AND CARDAMOM CAKE

Ingredients

- Ground almonds - 2 cups.
- Sugar - 1 cup.
- Cardamom powder - 1 teaspoon.
- Eggs - 4.
- Unsalted butter, melted - 1/2 cup.
- Almond slices for garnish.

Instructions

1. Preheat the oven to 180°C (350°F). Grease and flour an 8-inch round cake pan.

2. In a bowl, mix together ground almonds, sugar, and cardamom.

3. Beat in the eggs, one at a time, then stir in the melted butter.

4. Pour the batter into the prepared pan. Sprinkle the top with almond slices.

5. Bake for 25-30 minutes, or until a toothpick inserted into the center comes out clean.

6. Let cool before serving. Dust with powdered sugar if desired.

COCONUT DATE BALLS

Ingredients

- Dates, pitted - 2 cups.
- Shredded coconut - 1 cup.
- Almonds, finely chopped - 1/2 cup.
- Cardamom powder - 1/2 teaspoon.
- Additional shredded coconut for coating.

Instructions

1. In a food processor, blend the dates, 1 cup of shredded coconut, almonds, and cardamom until the mixture forms a sticky dough.

2. Take small amounts of the mixture and roll into balls.

3. Roll the balls in shredded coconut to coat.

4. Refrigerate for at least 1 hour before serving.

POMEGRANATE AND WALNUT DESSERT

Ingredients

- Pomegranate seeds - 1 cup.
- Walnuts, crushed - 1/2 cup.
- Honey - 2 tablespoons.
- Orange blossom water - 1 teaspoon.
- Ground cinnamon - 1/2 teaspoon.

Instructions

1. In a bowl, combine pomegranate seeds, crushed walnuts, honey, orange blossom water, and cinnamon.

2. Mix well until all ingredients are evenly distributed.

3. Chill in the refrigerator for 30 minutes before serving.

4. Serve in small bowls or glasses, garnished with a sprinkle of cinnamon or additional pomegranate seeds.

RECIPE INDEX

SALADS

RICE AND GRAINS

LAMB

BEEF

CHICKEN

SEAFOOD

BREADS

CONDIMENTS

DESSERTS

Printed in Great Britain
by Amazon

45740202R00116